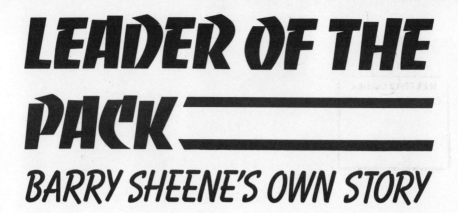

LEADER OF THE PACK

BARRY SHEENE'S OWN STORY

Barry Sheene
with Ian Beacham

Queen Anne Press
Macdonald & Co
London & Sydney

HERTFORDSHIRE
COUNTY LIBRARY

B | SHEENE

Hert

Queen Anne Press
Macdonald & Co
London & Sydney

© Barry Sheene 1983

First published in 1983 by Queen Anne Press,
a division of Macdonald & Co (Publishers) Ltd,
Maxwell House, 74 Worship Street, London EC2A 2EN.

Photographs reproduced by kind permission of Ian Beacham
with the following exceptions:

Plate ix (top): *CSS Promotions Ltd*
Plates xv (bottom) and xvi (bottom): *Richard Francis*
Plate i: *Nick Harris*
Plate vii (bottom): *Stewart Kendall*
Plates viii (bottom), x, xii (top)
and xiii (bottom): *Andrew Marriott*
Plates ix (bottom left and right) and xi: *Jon Reeves*
Plate viii (top): *The Sheene Family Collection*
Plates ii, iii and iv (top): *Syndication International*

All rights reserved. No part of this publication may be
reproduced, stored in a retrieval system, or transmitted
in any form or by any means electrical, mechanical,
photocopied or otherwise without the prior permission of
the publisher.

ISBN 0356 09412 X

Photoset by New Rush Filmsetters, London

Printed in Great Britain by Hazell, Watson & Viney Ltd.,
Aylesbury, Bucks

Contents

1
CRASH

As a big sign in my office proclaims, 'Today is the first day of the rest of my life', an expression I live by. What's the point of looking back? There's only the future to deal with.

Those who happened to be present that unforgettable afternoon of 28 July, mostly tradesfolk and pit crews with a sprinkling of Continental journalists, were stunned into silence as word spread within seconds that Sheene had crashed in a big way. The huge plume of tell-tale smoke that could be seen from all parts of the circuit said more about the disaster than the animated, garbled messages filtering throught the paddock. It was like some Red Indian smoke signal imparting bad news to the rest of the racing tribe.

Fellow riders, friends of Sheene who have shared the jibes and the jubilation that top-class motocycle racing seems to thrive upon, ran about aimlessly in the pandemonium that followed. Marco Lucchinelli, the previous year's world champion and a wildly passionate man in the classic Italian mould, was in a blind panic as he raced back to the Sheene camp shouting, 'Eez Barry, eez Barry. Get a helicopter. Quick, quick. We must get him to hospital.'

The strong feeling of brotherhood, the paddock togetherness, the unity of brave men, always comes to the surface when one of their own kind gets into trackside trouble. Now the professionals homed in on the debris to do what they could. Road racers can often be a better bet than a covey of track marshals with only a flimsy knowledge of medical matters when it comes to administering instant first aid at the scene of the bike pile-up.

The little man Roberts, who has raced about the place enough to know a bad case when he sees one, undertook the task of removing Sheene's AGV full-face helmet which, incredibly, bore only a few scrape marks.

It requires considerable skill to take off the helmet of a motionless rider correctly in order not to increase the risk of adding to any head injuries that might have occurred. But the risk exists of the rider choking, perhaps through having his tongue trapped in his wind-pipe, so the helmet has to be removed to gain access to the mouth. Kenny, Sheene's team-mate but still his greatest adversary and regarded as the most philoso-phical racer bike-racing has ever known, did his job ad-mirably, then stood aside while the experienced medical staff moved in.

Sheene's limp and seemingly lifeless body was stretch-ed out on the track surface in the weak sunshine well past the *Daily Express* bridge, getting on towards Woodcote Corner. The crash had taken place about 220 yards further back up the track.

The facts behind the pile-up quickly emerged. A West German, Alfred Weibel, had taken his 125cc MBA through Abbey Curve as fast as the little twin-cylinder Italian high-revver would go in fifth gear. The route he had taken was not a particularly text-book line and as he scurried through the curve doing the 'ton' he was right over to the right-hand side of the road with little room between him and the wide grass run-off area.

But trying to get through that narrow gap on his out-side was a French privateer, Patrick Igoa, whose much pacier 250 Yamaha scraped along the side of the MBA, tearing Weibel's leathers. The contact was sufficient to send Igoa onto the grass at the crown of the bend. He fell heavily, breaking his collarbone, and could do nothing to prevent his machine from careering back into the track.

Thirty seconds later, Sheene and the handsome red and white OW61 torpedoed Igoa's silent machine as it lay in ambush. The noise of two heavy metallic objects in collision boomed over the flat fields. The force of the impact was dreadful. The 250cc engine rocketed under the bridge as if fired from a gun, closely followed by the bouncing, bucking V-4. With 20 litres of 101-octane petrol on board, the first sparks ignited the fuel and transformed the catapulted machine into a fireball. Hurtling alongside this 160 mph Molotov cocktail was the black-leathered figure of Sheene, sliding more than 150 yards along the abrasive surface before coming to rest in an untidy, mangled heap. As he lay there motionless, it looked bad. Very bad. He could be dead, a disastrous termination to a brilliant career. The end of a truly incredible motorcycle racer: that was the immediate thought of car-mechanic Weibel who had pulled in by the bridge unhurt and was forced to watch Sheene cartwheel down the road. 'When I got to him I felt 100 per cent sure he was dead because he did not move,' he said later.

One-time 350cc world title holder Jon Ekerold was watching the closing stages of practice when he saw the tragedy unfold. He recalled to *Motor Cycle Weekly*: 'Igoa and his Yamaha ended up lying on the track. So I ran down the side to help him because he was not moving. As I ran towards him lots of riders passed the accident but after I had run about 50 yards, Barry hit Igoa's bike.

'There was a hell of a bang and I jumped back as the front end of Igoa's bike shot at me. It brushed my leg and I was lucky it didn't take it off.'

Meanwhile Middelburg, who broke a leg on the circuit in '79, ploughed through Igoa's stricken machine and finished up on the grass beyond the bridge with another broken leg.

The mass of debris could have come from an aeroplane disaster. Motorcycle components lay everywhere: an exploded fuel tank here; a dismembered frame there. The carcass of Sheene's V-4, all that was left of what was probably the greatest racing motorcycle to come out of Yamaha's Iwata race shop, ended its manic jour-

ney not far from Sheene's limp body. It was minus front
wheel, fairing, tank and a hundred other bits. With the
fire extinguished, the white powder-covered remains
looked as if they'd been embalmed ready for burial.

After Roberts' intervention, a gaggle of helpers surrounded Sheene, their faces stricken. Marie Armes, wife
of the chief paddock marshal and a former nurse, had
sped to the battlefield by car on hearing the devastating
news. Barry was still breathing though unconscious but
she took the precaution of inserting a breathing-aid tube
into his mouth.

Barry's father Frank, who fashioned his son's career
and never misses an opportunity to see his boy ride winners, grabbed a passing rider on a Suzuki, and beseech-
ed him to rush him across the pit roads to the scene of
the destruction.

Said Frank, 'As soon as I saw the crowds of people on
the track, I knew there was trouble. But no-one seemed
quite sure what to do. They appeared to be just standing
about. I knelt down and shouted: "Barry, Barry — can
you hear me?" He mumbled something like "Urrgh,
Dad..." and I let out a massive sigh of relief. At least he's
still with us, I thought. It seemed ages before he went
into the ambulance and then into the circuit medical
centre. He looked deathly white, far worse than when
we picked him up after Daytona. In the confusion and
panic, people were shouting at the medical staff to hurry
up. But with everyone worrying about whether or not
he would survive, it was a natural reaction to want to
have him taken to a hospital where there would be complete facilities.'

When she heard the dreadful news, Stephanie Maclean, Barry's girlfriend, frantically sped on a mini-bike
to the wreckage of man and machine. The sight filled
her with fear. Her loved one, the guy with whom she
had spent seven happy years travelling from one race
meeting to the next, was lying in an untidy heap surrounded by a sea of worried faces. 'Bloody hell,' was her
first reaction. She began to shake so much that Martyn

Ogborne, team manager of the HB Suzuki works team, began to hold her arms. 'I thought Barry was ready to pop off,' she recalled. 'But I knew once we got him to hospital, everthing would sort itself out.'

Anxiety for Barry's well-being intensified amongst his racing colleagues when there seemed to be an interminable time-lag between the accident and medical help arriving. Special care was taken so as not to add to his injuries while he was loaded on to a stretcher. It was immediately obvious that the circuit's own medical centre, sophisticated though its facilities are in comparison to some GP circuits, was of little use in this situation. Barry was replaced in the ambulance for the drive to the emergency unit of Northampton General Hospital. 'I was so relieved when I was told by the doctor that everything would heal and was just thankful he hadn't hurt his head,' said Stephanie, a former model. 'But it never occurred to me to even suggest to Barry that he think about the future. Whatever decision he makes he will reach it by himself and neither his parents nor I would dream of putting any pressure on him to make him give up racing.'

With Sheene in the ambulance went his girlfriend Stephanie, Mrs Armes, his Venezuelan buddy Roberto Pietri and a circuit doctor. Sheene began to regain consciousness on the journey and the agony of the pain coming from two shattered legs and a smashed left arm must have been indescribable. He began, for some reason, to shout in Spanish — one of three foreign languages he has taught himself to speak fluently — and then boomed out: 'For fuck sake someone give me a cigarette!' He was making progress!

Never for one moment did I wane in my belief that I could win the world 1982 500cc world championship. My spirits, my morale, my determination...they were all sky-high throughout the season as my ambitions locked on to that target. All that remained was to ensure that everything else came together — the results, the reliability of the bikes and reasonable good fortune. Sadly, it wasn't to work out that way.

I didn't regard myself as a full-time factory runner — I was just a guy who had a contract with the UK importers of Yamaha, Mitsui, to ride semi-works bikes. That has always been my arrangement with Yamaha. Kenny Roberts was their main man and, consequently, he would always have preferential treatment over the latest equipment.

Not many people know this, but to fund my racing effort for 1982 I had to raise cash by selling my blue Porsche 928S and my Piper Aztec aeroplane which I had had for about five years. The Piper Aztec, a twin-engined six seater capable of flying from Gatwick to Nice non-stop, was sometimes used to get me to race meetings abroad but normally it was hired out for charter work to bring me in extra income.

As it was more important to make a success of my racing, those two luxury items seemed dispensable.

I could have signed for Giacomo Agostini's Marlboro team at the beginning of '82. He would have paid me a good salary and I would not have had to foot the bill for the mechanics, transporters and the host of other annual expenses. But I knew that that arrangement wouldn't be too successful.

I wanted to run my own team, even though it would earn me less money. So I told Ago I wasn't keen on riding for an Italian team. I'm a true Brit and much prefer to base my organisation in a 900-year-old village that is typically English. The emphasis had to be British, although we couldn't do much about the origin of the bikes. That's why I approached John Player, a traditional British company, for financial backing.

To be truthful, the money paid to me by John Player in '82 did not amount to much. What they gave me in cash terms was only enough to pay half the expenses of the racing team but I had signed for them believing it was an investment for the future. I have made better investments in my time!

I had been waiting for the new Yamaha V-4 all year. It was a machine which offered substantial improvements on the conventional 'square-four' Yamaha I had been riding, the most important being better acceleration when the needle was halfway round the tacho. By paying a lot of attention to careful frame construction, the Japanese had made the new Yamaha bike a lighter bike than mine and the saving of a few pounds here and there can make all the difference to a bike's competitiveness. It was pretty clear that the V-4 was generally a better bike than my OW60.

It seemed that Kenny Roberts, a sturdily-built American with three world championships behind him, had been given the V-4 in one last desperate effort to keep him racing for Yamaha in '82, which he intended to make his last season in Europe, provided he could go out at the top. The V-4, Yamaha told him, would be the machine to take the title.

One of the problems with the standard square-four arrangement — a concept lovingly cherished by Suzuki, Kawasaki and Yamaha — is that the quartet of side-facing carburettors prevent the motor being mounted low in the chassis and increase the width of the full fibre-glass fairing.

With the V-4 configuration, the engine could be positioned lower in the alloy space frame with the two disc valves and carburettors placed between the two banks of cylinders. Guillotine-type exhaust power valves were meant to broaden the power band.

We suspected power output would be something like 125 brake horsepower at 10,500 rpm, but the beauty of this slimmer and lighter 250-pound bike, as I saw it, was that many of the heavier parts were concentrated near to the centre of gravity, making it simpler to flick the machine from side to side — so critical when taking chicanes at speed.

Weight distribution is a key element in producing a bike that handles well. The frame of the V-4 had been set forward to put more weight over the front wheel which would help to keep the front end from pawing the air on acceleration. (Back in the seventies, when I rode the 650cc Suzuki, one of my favourite machines because of its wide power band, I added a 15-pound weight to the front to make it a better balanced motorcycle.)

The V-4, on paper, had everything going for it. A lot of thought and effort had gone into its construction and Kenny should have counted his blessings. I only wished Yamaha had presented me with one at the same time.

Kenny had been allocated the new bike in April and I had to make do with the previous year's machine until Yamaha felt the time was right to let me have one. A strange move, I thought, because the Yamaha factory's race department competes with the aim of winning; yet it seemed that in their eyes, this flyer developed in Japan as a potential world-beater could be ridden successfully only by one man.

Unfortunately for me, the technicians felt that man had to be Kenny, instead of believing, as I did, that two heads would be better than one. Their faith in Kenny seemed unshakeable.

Their tunnel vision surprised me. Although he may be an absolutely brilliant rider, Kenny's knowledge of how to set up a racing bike is limited, to say the least. Like hundreds of other riders today, he can detect something alarmingly wrong with a bike after a few laps. But to pinpoint the problem accurately, and to suggest possible remedies to his mechanics, is beyond him.

You can only build a better bike with the help of knowledge gained from someone riding it to its maximum, then reporting back on how it fared. This is not one of Kenny's strong points.

Kenny's shortcomings in this department were emphasised, so far as I was concerned, in 1981, when we both rode the OW54 for Yamaha. From the day I got that square four to the end of the season, the machine was improving all the time. Changes, I reckoned, needed to be made as soon as I was given the bike, and we put a lot of hard work into altering various of its characteristics. The Japanese translated my comments into positive action, and trouble-spots such as poor handling were virtually eliminated by the end of the season. Yet Kenny, using the same model which had been honed and perfected throughout the season by technicians acting on my recommendations, claimed the initial problems never disappeared. The bike, according to him, had shown no improvement all season!

It's all very well to say something's not right with a bike; but that's just half of the problem. The important function of any racer employed to develop a motorcycle is to state exactly why there is a problem. It flabbergasted me to discover that Kenny was unable to diagnose the cause of trouble. The 1981 season proved a real eye-opener and, as far as I was concerned, made a mockery of some people's claims that Yamaha had the ideal test rider in Kenny.

Having said that, I must reiterate that Kenny is a remarkable racer, as his results in Europe prove, and perhaps there is no-one more accomplished in adapting to a new bike. I, on the other hand, prefer to have a new machine adapted and tailored to conform to my requirements.

I suppose that Kenny deserved to have the new V-4 for 1982 first, if only because of his loyalty. He had been with Yamaha for years and was their number one man. I could never have said to Yamaha, 'Give me the new bike, not Kenny'. I wasn't in any position to dictate to them. But if they wanted to get back some reasonable information on how their new baby performed and what areas needed vital attention, it didn't make sense to rely on Kenny.

There was no doubt that I would get a V-4 at some stage of the season, but as to when, the Yamaha boys said they weren't sure, So it was a case of soldiering on with the previous year's model, to which I didn't object, since I knew its capabilities after completing the 1981 season in pleasing style, winning a Grand Prix and lots of international events.

The Japanese normally send for their contracted road racers in the early part of winter to try out the modified machines on their own test circuit at Iwata. This allows time for major changes to the chassis or engine to be made before the Grand Prix campaign commences the following spring. Kenny got the call first and he put both the new V-4 and the revamped square four which had been built with him in mind, through their paces. Everything was OK, he said, including the handling. Fine.

I decided to turn down an invitation from Japan to test the square four because I couldn't see any point in riding the bike over there on a Monday and then having it crated up to come to Europe on the Thursday. Even if I had found anything wrong with it, there would be no time left to make changes. There seemed little point in trekking over to the far side of the world when there was no way I could influence the way the bike was set up.

When the bike eventually arrived in England, I took it to Donington Park for testing and in just four laps in the rain I could tell that the head angle was completely wrong and the castor and trail angles were such that reasonable handling was out of the question. The frame geometry appeared a complete balls-up.

That same night I phoned the head man at Yamaha's race shop in Japan to explain the alteration I needed to have done to the bike. 'But Kenny says bike OK,' he replied. I said I didn't care what Kenny said. I knew it was wrong. Without a new frame for the first round in Argentina, I told him, there was no point in my racing there.

All credit to the boys at Yamaha. They constructed a fresh frame designed with the angles I requested and it was air-freighted to Buenos Aires just before the Grand Prix. The position of the foot-rests, inch perfect for Kenny's short legs, remained unchanged, though, and that did give us a bit of a headache. Because of the distance to Argentina, we were unable to take a lot of regular equipment including oxy-acetylene cutters so I dashed into Buenos Aires to find an aluminium welding plant. The factory hands were on holiday but I slapped some money into the outstretched hands of the owners, and they allowed me use of the gear to re-weld the foot-rests in the right place to accommodate my longer legs.

All these changes had the desired effect. In spite of other factory runners from Honda and Suzuki having been at the Argentinian circuit for some time, testing and setting-up their machines to suit the track, which I had seen for the first time only a few days earlier, I managed to put in the fastest time in the opening practice session. In all four practice sessions I wasn't out of the leading four. I proved the bike had been put back into shape.

But as time went by in '82, I realised I had to have that V-4 to be on equal terms with Kenny. I continued to badger away at the Yamaha engineers, only to be told I wouldn't receive my new machine until Kenny was happy. I pointed out, as politely as I could, that Kenny's inability to distinguish good from bad in terms of changes needed to be made to the machine would mean he would never be totally happy with it. The wait was going to be a long one!

But whatever I thought or felt, the fact remained I was still number two in the queue to get a ride on the V-4. Or so I thought! But during the summer of '82 an Italian journalist, one of many hundreds from that country covering road racing, informed me Graeme Crosby had tested the machine at Mugello, news which immediately made me dial Yamaha in Japan for some explanation. I was told that Crosby just happened to be in Italy at the time, the bike was Kenny's spare and in any case the gearchange was not on the right-hand side.

I soon discovered that Crosby, in fact, was staying in England and had flown to Mugello specially for the test, and the bike, incredibly, was the one earmarked for me. It didn't make sense and I had to put it down to unfathomable Japanese logic.

Then at the next Grand Prix at Rijeka in Yugoslavia, I spotted this very same V-4, complete and ready to run, strapped inside one of the Yamaha transporters. I made polite appeals to take the bike away with me to England to allow ample time to familiarise myself with it prior to the first outing at the British Grand Prix at Silverstone. No, they said. No V-4 until the start of Silverstone race week. Orders.

I still wonder what might have been the course of events during that period in late July had I received the 'vee' earlier.

There would have been adequate time to try it out effectively, check its characteristics, iron out any problems, and modify all those parts which would have been designed with Kenny in mind. You can never spend too much time getting to grips with a new bike. Gearing, carburations, tyres, plugs, suspension...the list of mechanical tinkering is endless once the bike's quirks and idiosyncrasies have been established.

It was 9.30 am on the Monday of Silverstone race week when I finally took delivery of the new model. That left a mere three days of testing before qualifying commenced for the British GP, no time at all. But I knew there was nothing else I could do but make the most of every minute of practice available to me. I realised I was going to have to hustle and push my chief mechanic Ken Fletcher and his spannermen all the time. Any changes I needed would have to be made at record speed and in addition they were not too familiar with the set-up of this type of cylinder configuration.

What added to the pressure was the importance of the event. The British GP is, for me, the most significant race meeting of the year. To ride well in front of your own fans provides a satisfaction unobtainable at many other events. The British crowd at Silverstone is traditionally large and patriotically boisterous. And if there's a chance of a Brit riding his balls off to finish amongst the leaders, the fervour of the spectators can transmit itself to the rider.

Through one reason or another, I have not won a Grand Prix in Britain, though I came close in '79, when Kenny just kept his nose in front in what must still be one of the best-remembered finishes of all time. But I have always set my heart on getting that first place. As well as the personal kudos, I knew that if I could win it would do so much for the sagging fortunes of motorcycling sport in Britain. The crowd were coming to see me do so well and if I could deliver, 80,000 people would go home encouraged to turn out for another meeting later in the year.

As I was the only British rider with a cat in hell's chance of winning, I was desperately hoping everything would work out right this time: no engine trouble; no bad starts; no freak weather conditions; and no accidents, although I have always said it would have to be something outside my control for me to get involved in a crash. I don't ride to fall; I'm always within my safety limits and I know precisely what the bike and I together are capable of. Any misfortune that might happen would be, I believed, the result of an outside factor: oil on the track, an engine seizure, a puncture or even someone else falling in my path.

But all my thoughts were positive. My riding was calm, collected, as good as at any time, and I was in a superb position to make a late bid for the 500cc title. It had been a good season for me on the conventional Yamaha and the prospects of it being an even better year were increasing as the days went by to the Silverstone. I just felt in my blood that I could go on to win the championship in '82. The rest of the circuits after Silverstone were ones I liked and it was often the case that I finished stronger in the latter half of the season than many of my rivals. Whether some lose interest or their determination wanes is a matter for conjecture but I am just as red-hot keen as when I begin the season.

The great thing was that the specialist press saw the title race as between Franco Uncini and Roberts, with me as the rank outsider, even though I was lying second in the points table. That was ideal, because it took a lot of pressure away from me. While the attention was focused on those two, I could dedicate myself to winning the series without, for the moment, being bothered by the glare of publicity.

I knew that Uncini's Suzuki had to break down once in those final four Grands Prix to allow me to have a chance. But the law of averages in racing told me that his bike couldn't go a whole season without having a few mechanical disasters. I had broken down during the year, as had Kenny. Surely it was soon the turn of Franco and his Suzuki. When that happened, it would substantially improve my chances of making up that 20-point gap, or so I thought. Or I perhaps could collect sufficient points at Silverstone, Anderstorp, Mugello and Hockenheim and hope he came in well down the field on a couple of occasions. It's easy to kid other people. But not yourself, and I believed I had a damn good chance of becoming champion, for the third time.

Everyone seemed to sense this could at last be my turn to win the home GP and the media coverage I received in the run-up was incredible. The amount of interest this race was generating surpassed anything in motorcycling history, it seemed, and I was pleased that my contribution would help to increase the appeal and excitement of road racing. Of added significance was the fact the 500cc race was to be televised live. To perform and to succeed in front of an audience of millions presented me with a marvellous opportunity, and I intended to make the most of it.

But first I had to develop an affinity with the new bike.

2
PRELUDE
TO DISASTER

With a quick push and a bump, the V-4 burst into life in my eager hands as I started it up for the first time. It was Monday morning, Silverstone's special practice day for factory 500cc riders. I eased her on to the track and past the deserted grandstand. Now it was time to learn what she was made of. A few laps later I had to come in, acutely aware of glaring errors in the chassis geometry made obvious by the way in which she handled. Disappointment must have been written all over my face.

When I queried the head angle set-up with the Japanese engineer in my pit garage, he said it was precisely the same as on my square-four machine. As I felt this wasn't true, I measured the weight distribution of both bikes front and back on a pair of bathroom scales we carry in our 16-ton Daf transporter and discovered they were almost identical. But a check of the head angle of the V-4 revealed it to be three degrees too steep. Even half a degree out is noticeable; three degrees is absolute insanity. It makes the bike feel hopelessly wrong to race at speed.

Swift surgery was vital if I wanted to race this machine. I told Ken Fletcher to strip the bike and I went off to phone Spondon Engineering at Derby to ask them if they could modify the frame and alter the head angle, which they happily agreed to do. The frame was returned the following evening in time for the machine to be rebuilt overnight ready for the Wednesday open practice session.

The Yamaha technicians who had been surprised to discover the oversight in the head angle seemed quite happy for me to make the necessary changes and I know they must have appreciated the wisdom of my action when I put in a 1

minute 30 seconds time on my first real flying lap of the day.
The bike felt very much better and I believed it was capable
of improving on this time which was just outside the 500cc
lap record.

Carburation changes were next. I wanted to try different
carb settings because there seemed room for improvement in
the mid-range power band. All four carbs came off, were
stripped and inspected. The setting was changed slightly but
the Yamaha engineers were puzzled when the carbs kept
flooding with fuel each time we restarted the bike. As they
played around with the carburation, vital minutes slipped by.
Meanwhile, I told Ken Fletcher to switch the gear ratios to
suit the corners on the track.

I kept thinking of what I might have done in the Grands
Prix if I had had the V-4 machine from the word go. I knew
now what I had been up against. This was a supreme motorcycle with ferocious mid-range acceleration. It was perhaps
no quicker than my old bike when flat out but it had that
vital extra power; phenomenally better in the middle range. I
would have been OK soldiering on with the old model but,
boy, I knew this one was going to make life so much easier.

By 3pm, I began to get edgy. There was little left of the
day's practice session and my pit crew were still buggering
around trying to find the cause of the flooding. I said, 'Come
on, we've got to get this thing right — there's hardly any
practice time left.'

I could have put in a few more quick laps in the morning
session but there were so many other riders on the circuit it
was like trying to negotiate Piccadilly Circus in the rush
hour. It was difficult to get a clear run there. Valuable
seconds would be lost going round a bunch of slower lads.
Most people know by now that machines from the humble
125cc right through the capacity spectrum to 1000cc were
allowed out on the track at the same time. But it was not just
the varying speeds of the bikes that made practice a hazardous business. Riders of enormously different abilities, from
world champion to club novice, were given the chance to mix
it out there on one of Europe's fastest tracks. And I certainly
wasn't going to take any risks. That's not part of my racing

philosophy.

At last the machine was back together again, but the modifications to the frame and carbs were just the tip of the iceberg. There were so many other aspects of setting up that had to be worked on. It's one thing perfecting the bike so that it doesn't shake or wobble, for instance; it's another ensuring the wheels don't patter. It's a mammoth job ironing out the wrinkles with a new machine when you've less than a week in which to do it. The only way I was going to discover where we could make those necessary changes was to make that bike fly — there was no other way of ensuring that we would go into Sunday's big race with a motorcycle correctly prepared and thoroughly tested, a bike minutely examined to make it run quickly, smoothly and reliably. The final ten minutes of the practice session were desperately important. I could have learned just one lesson, made this one vital change that could make this machine a winner.

I rode up to the track entrance barrier to be told by the official controlling the gate there were just two laps left before the day's session came to a halt.

In spite of my anger at the number of riders allowed out on the track, I had to join them. With the official timed practice to assign the grid positions beginning on the Friday the amount of work that needed to be done on the bike made it essential to go out. I had to get the difficult testing work out of the way. There was no option.

Had I been like everyone else, forced to pay the Silverstone fee of £22, I would have considered the day to be exceedingly poor value for money. But I hadn't paid because no-one asked me to. Nor had I signed a single form — including the disclaimer which absolves the circuit from any blame in the event of a mishap. No one asked me to produce any documents before I was allowed out on the track.

Even at this late stage of the afternoon, the volume of traffic was undiminished. Becoming frustrated by the constant stream of machines flashing by, I held back until there was a break in the flow of riders of whom, according to a radio report by the late Jock Taylor, as many as 80 were circulating at one time. Looking to my left, I spotted the Dutchman Jack

Middelburg coming through, so I thought it would be a good idea to link up with him. At least I knew him to be safe and he would be taking similar lines to me. The vast difference in speeds between say, a 500 like mine and a 125, would mean I might come into a bend behind another rider 35 mph quicker, sometimes even faster if the guy was a dunce. The biggest problem was having to roll off the power if he was on your line. You'd see him ahead of you and you wouldn't have a clue as to his intentions.

I must have passed a few as my first flying lap was a good one, around 1.30 again I was told... much, much later. At 117 mph I was apparently only a whisker outside the lap record I had set up in '79. I knew that if I could squeeze in one last lap I could go faster, which would have blitzed the record and get the tongues wagging. The bike was feeling really good.

I could guess it was a good lap time because of the way the bike felt. Regular glances at the rev counter told me how the motor was pulling at various sections of the course and gave an indication of the kind of pace I was maintaining. Of course I had no speedometer on the bike, just tachometer and temperature gauges. In practice I don't bother with pit signal boards to show previous lap times as others do. The main thing is to have the bike sorted out; lap times are of secondary importance. The water-cooled V-4 was revving to 11,300 rpm, nothing out of the ordinary. The tyres were the standard off-the-peg Michelin slick, exactly the same as I had used at Silverstone the year before. I knew they were perfectly suited for Silverstone. Within a lap they had warmed up to their ideal operating temperature and were gripping well.

Everything was on course. The track was dry and there was only a slight breeze to ruffle the flags along the start-and-finish straight. Middelburg was still ahead of me, but looked ready for taking. So I squeezed by him at the end of Hangar Straight, outbraking him into Stowe Corner and going up inside him. I never forgot that corner, Crosby had brought me and Lucchinelli off there the year before.

Coming out of the right-hand Club Corner heading towards Abbey Curve, I quickly glanced over my shoulder for a millisecond to check on where Jack was. He had won Silverstone the previous year and I guessed he wouldn't be too far off my tail. In fact I'd put about 20 or 30 yards between us by then.

I was then perfectly lined up for the ultra-fast gentle left-hand kink of Abbey Curve. As I screamed round the curve I gave a split-second thought as to how the bike's tail behaved at that point of the circuit. I wanted to see if the bike shook coming out of the bend. I can remember thinking that a slight modification to the tail wouldn't go amiss.

My chin was down on the tank as I went into Abbey Curve. All you can see then is the top of the *Daily Express* bridge. So that's what you aim for. Your eye-line heads straight for the tip of that big bridge because it's a blind rise. You cannot see anything until you've passed the crest. Well, with your head down, you can see 30 feet in front of you at best.

I came over the crest of the rise on my usual line and there was a bike lying in the road and I hit it. Then all I can recall seeing was a big ball of flame. Nothing else. That was all there was to it. What happened next is still a complete mystery to me. My recollection of the impact was, and still is, nil. All I can remember was coming round in hospital some time later.

Just as you come up to Woodcote, the bike is doing its absolute maximum, about 175 mph. So in terms of speed, I could only have chosen Hangar Straight as a worse place to have an accident. And had that bike been lying anywhere else on the track, I could have spotted it, even without a marshal's assistance, and taken evasive action.

But I saw no marshals before everything happened in the stretch leading up to the Abbey Curve. If Igoa's crash occurred as has been reported, well before Jack and I arrived there, where were the warning flags? When I rode out during the morning session I was not aware of a shortage of flag marshals but, there again, you don't notice these guys until something goes wrong.

I had earlier made my feelings known to a lot of people about the volume of riders and the lack of segregation of classes. 'Somebody is going to get killed if they're not careful,' I remember remarking to my father and some others and I was quoted to that effect in a motorcycling magazine. It was just f****** madness. Representations by other parties were made, I understand, to Silverstone officials to reduce the numbers. I still find it incredible that some of the riders were not even entered for the British Grand Prix. How could I be anything but bitter about the fact that anyone with £22 in his pocket could go along to Silverstone on that day and take a racing bike out?

The biggest irony of the whole, sickening drama was that, after being for so long a campaigner for improved safety throughout the world, I should almost have my legs dismembered on a track previously regarded as being one of the safer circuits.

Two former world champions and as knowledgeable as they come on safety matters were emphatic about the cause of the accident, when interviewed on BBC radio. Giacomo Agostini, eight times a 500cc world title holder, raged, 'I think the organisers were very stupid to put all the classes together. This was very bad.'

And Kenny Roberts was even more critical. 'Any fool knows you don't put 125s out with 500s. I almost ran into three or four 125s, so it was a big problem. I just think riders are really foolish for going out there — and I'm one of them. So we got what we deserved. We were out there riding and we shouldn't have been.' Roberts, in fact, admitted he would have refused to go out there to practice had he not had to scrub in two new Dunlop slick tyres.

So long as they held an international competition licence, any rider, it seemed, could have enjoyed the Wednesday practice free-for-all, if the experience of 19-year-old Kim Barker from Lincoln is anything to go by. He relates, 'I heard there was an unofficial practice and I was hoping to get a start in the 125cc Grand Prix. So I came to practice to get my bike set up just in case I was given a start on the Friday. I went to the office, paid my £22, and I was out on the circuit practising.'

Barker claims that no documents were checked. He was

asked only to sign a piece of paper, which he thought to be a receipt. This was given, together with a helmet sticker to indicate he had paid his dues. He maintains no-one checked whether he was a GP competitor or, in fact, whether he even possessed a licence to ride. Luckily, he had a full international licence, for he could have been just a beginner.

But the Silverstone circuit's then press and promotion officer, Mark Cole, was adamant that their system of only allowing Grand Prix competitors out on the Wednesday practice day was almost fool-proof. 'We only accepted entrants for the Grand Prix,' he is on record as saying. 'Silverstone circuit would not permit any testing by anyone who was not an official entry in the Grand Prix. The entry being accepted for the Grand Prix by the Auto-Cycle Union, then that man must have a full international licence.'

Mr Cole added that the programme would have been checked to ensure the rider had an entry in the GP. Told that Kim Barker had not been allocated a place amongst the qualifiers, Mr Cole was surprised it had happened but added it had no bearing on my accident.

Speaking on the same radio broadcast, Mr Cole said, 'You can't blame the organisation for a simple accident. It was a simple accident. A man fell off his motorcycle on the track. The bike was lying in the track and before anything could be done about moving it — we're talking about a matter of perhaps ten seconds — Barry Sheene and Jack Middelburg arrived on the scene. Sheene, for some reason, hit the wreckage. Middelburg got involved as well.

'I don't think any of the blame lies with Silverstone any more than it would lie with Barry Sheene for hitting a bike lying on the track.

'They fully knew the risks of mixing with the smaller machines. Having said that, of course, this accident — this very, very unfortunate accident about which we are all very upset — obviously had no bearing on the fact that bikes are mixed up. The fact was, someone had fallen off a bike in the track. It could have been a 500 bike, it could have been anything. No matter what capacity it was, it would have had the same effect.'

Jock Taylor, riders' representative to the FIM at the time and 1980 sidecar world champion before his untimely death on the Finnish Imatra circuit just 18 days after my incident, was critical of the numbers of machines allowed out on the track, a figure he estimated at 80.

Silverstone disputed that number, with Mr Cole claiming that only 80 bikes had signed on for testing, 20 of which were sidecars, and he thought it very unlikely that at any time during the day all 60 would be out simultaneously.

He added, 'The ACU, for qualifying, allow 50 bikes on the track for one qualifying session. We doubt if we even had that many on the track for this private test session. But they also realise they are also out there testing; they're not practicing, they're not trying to set a fast time. They're just setting their bikes up.'

In reply to the comment that riders were obviously trying to set fast times on some laps, Mr Cole replied, 'That's up to the riders. It's like any test day we have at Silverstone. You come here to test — you're trying to qualify. You should be bedding-in brakes, checking tyres. Of course, you're out to do one or two quick laps like you would do in car Grand Prix racing but normally you wait for a gap in the traffic. I must reiterate, the fact that these bikes are mixed up had no bearing at all on this accident.'

I have to say Mr Cole knew next to nothing about testing bikes. There's only one way accurately to monitor a bike's performance — and that's to take it up to racing speeds where all the components are being worked to their full potential.

Jock Taylor claimed that some of the bikes in what he termed the 'sheer procession' were doing 60 mph slower than the fast men and he added, 'I've always stressed there should be an extra day's practice for a Grand Prix and it should be the country's controlling body who organises it and not the circuit. In other words, there should be three days' practice with controlled times for each. But times in that free practice should not count toward qualifying. That way there's no mix-up of speeds.'

Jock pointed out he had made that same recommendation at the previous year's FIM Congress in Japan but it had been rejected. He intended raising the matter again at the 1982 FIM annual gathering in Yugoslavia and felt confident the extra day of controlled practice for Grand Prix would at last be granted.

On a glass-like road surface made tortuous by heavy rain his three-wheeler outfit thudded into a telegraph pole in the Finnish GP at considerable speed. The popular Taylor lay in his home-town cemetery before the FIM delegates could hear what would have been an impassioned yet well-reasoned and justifiable plea for action.

But even though it was an open practice day, there should have been a marshal on duty at the section, especially as it is virtually a blind bend. Now I've always been regarded as a safety-minded competitor and I would be the first to slow down when a yellow flag is waved about. Where was it that afternoon at Silverstone?

The very fact that Jon Ekerold was running down the track to assist when he saw Igoa crash must indicate there weren't enough marshals on duty.

Apparently I was fairly coherent in the ambulance but I can't recall anything about the journey, though I do remember talking to Steph in hospital about the operation due to take place that same evening.

By all accounts, I went 30 feet skywards and was projected probably 100 yards through the air before hitting the ground, ending up almost 300 yards from where I crashed. Looking at it realistically, I have to say I was fortunate to escape with the injuries I received. I was let off lightly. I had only to land on my head to break my neck. I could have hit the bike and broken my back through whiplash. Yes, I suppose Somebody up there was looking after me. Logically, if you're doing 180 mph and smash into something lying in the track, you've a bloody good chance of hurting yourself, hurting yourself very badly. But then so has the ordinary road rider going at 30 mph when he smacks into a car pulling out of a side road. He has just as much chance of breaking his body.

When I finally came to my senses in hospital and was told the full story about the accident, I immediately said to

Stephanie and Franco (my father) that there couldn't have been marshals at that point. I know what I'm like with marshals; experience has taught me to obey their every flag command. In the Dutch TT at Assen a few weeks previously, the crossed flags were put out to indicate that the race had been stopped because of the torrential rain and I pulled up as per the rule book. I categorically state there was absolutely no warning as to what was going on. Two feet to the left or right and I would have missed the fallen bike, yet Jon told me that even though people ran up waving their arms to warn the next wave of riders some way off they still had a hell of a job in avoiding the debris from my accident.

People have asked me if I felt the pain when I tumbled end over end. But I cannot recall feeling a thing. My only memory is the vision of fire. In the impact I must have slid forward and crunched the fuel-tank with my knees, balls or whatever and then the tank exploded. As I shot forward, my knees smashed into the handlebars and my left knee broke my left wrist and crushed the hand while it was still wrapped around the rubber grip. Being a left-hand corner, my left knee would have been sticking out slightly and would have therefore have been closer to the bars. That's why that side of my body came off worst.

I suppose the strength of my special knee-protector pads caused my smashed knuckles, as both knee and hand impacted. With my long legs, my knees always sit high on a bike, and so, being on the same level, the knee coming forward must have snapped the wrist.

The bars struck my legs just half an inch below the knee protectors. Higher, and I'm sure there would have been no breaks. I had these pads made in Japan out of plastic, backed with foam rubber, and I reckon I was the first to use them in 1976. They are designed to protect against impact when the knee scrapes the tarmac on cornering, and I guess they are so strong they could be hit with a huge hammer and still show no sign of damage.

Apart from my normal riding gear, the only other safety feature I always wear is my home-made back protector, made from special three-quarter inch foam and designed to absorb impact. That worked, because there was positively no damage to my back. Incredible really, because someone on the central runway in the middle of the circuit looked up upon hearing the explosion and saw me loop so high in the air he thought I was certain to hit the bridge. The lack of scrapes on my leather suggest I must have sailed through the air for a good hundred yards.

Some might jib at wearing a back protector because it makes them look out of shape or fat, but I couldn't give two hoots about appearances when my personal well-being is at stake.

Over my whole body there was only a handful of grazes to be seen, which I have to attribute to the thickness of my Italian Dainese leathers that I have made to 2½mm thickness in preference to the normal ¾mm. Some might regard the extra weight of hide as a drawback but it doesn't handicap me in any way. First priority has to be the protection of your skin and body. It's true my heavier leathers — sewn together with special catgut stitching — make me really warm during a GP in a hot country but I can put up with any amount of heat. The important thing is that they don't impede arm or leg movements, so when I come out of an accident like that one without even so much as a skin burn, they've got to be the right clothing to wear. There wasn't a tear anywhere, just a pair of compression marks below the knees where the bars struck.

Now didn't that helmet stand the test? It was pretty badly grazed, but the only thing that broke off was one of the special extra-strong visor studs on the side. I get AGV to put these on so the visor remains in place for as long as possible if you are thrown along the road. It means the eyes are being protected for a greater period of time.

Somehow a burst of flame must have got into the helmet under the chin section because my eye-lashes were singed off. At the scene of the accident, apparently, I must have wiped my blood-covered pulped hand across my face when they removed my lid and so latecomers immediately suspected I had suffered facial injuries or, as my mother believed, that I had serious internal bleeding.

The leather gauntlet-type gloves I wear have also been made for maximum protection In the event of a backward slide, the long wrist section continues to cover the lower forearm and won't come off to expose bare flesh that could rub along the tarmac. But one of my fingers was hit so hard, it virtually exploded, blowing out the fingernail. As the glove was still intact, I knew later there was only one place that fingernail could be. I cut the glove apart, and sure enough, there was the complete fingernail together with fleshy parts of the finger.

All in all, my gear stood up well to this ultimate track test. What was inside the equipment didn't do quite as well! But I have always insisted on having the very best in equipment: helmets, leathers and boots that I can trust in the event of a bad moment. It would not change my attitude one bit to be offered a billion pounds to wear a particular brand: if I felt the goods were not up to scratch, I would not wear them. My survival comes first. It pays to be fussy and I wouldn't want some youngster to buy that same unsatisfactory tackle with his confidence in the product bolstered by the fact that Barry Sheene felt it was good enough.

Perhaps the slice of luck I had in surviving lay in the fact that I was wearing my normal Gary Nixon tee-shirt — one of several my old American buddy gave me — and the trusty blue underpants. As older fans of mine know, I wear the blue for racing because I think they act as a good-luck charm. Nixon — one-time Suzuki works racer — gave me a pile of his own tee-shirts years ago and as I started winning with them on, I maintained the habit. I was in blue when I came a purler at Daytona in 1975 and got away with just a badly broken leg, shoulder and arm.

Around my neck hung my lucky FIM 750cc European Championship medal, dating from 1973, which I always have attached to a silver chain when I'm racing, together with my 'fica' charm from Brazil, an ivory symbol of virility.

I believe a lot in luck. Steph's former mother-in-law is a professional clairvoyant and after studying my birth-sign at the beginning of '82, she issued a warning to me to take care on dates that add to a figure with a one in the number. I crashed at Silverstone on the 28th which, added together, produce a figure containing one. Well it might have been a coincidence, but who knows?

My marvellous surgeon, Nigel Cobb, took one look at the X-rays and realised that this was a really severe case. A lot of his work had been taken up dealing with motorway smashes from the nearby M1 and he knew a bad case when he saw one. The legs, he said, were held on to the upper parts of the limbs by the arteries almost alone, the bones and ligaments had been smashed so badly.

Now, I have been racing long enough to know that accidents can and will happen. Even to me. So I have always told Stephanie and Franco never to allow anyone, anywhere, to cut off a part of my body, no matter how bad the injury is. They knew the score.

But Dad hadn't heard of Nigel Cobb before and was concerned as to how good he was. He was keen to check his references with someone he knew, like Ernie Kirwin in London who did a brilliant repair job when I smashed my left knee in the seventies. He instructed Steve Parrish, my constant companion, to phone Ernie, who without a second thought said, 'You couldn't have a better guy to work on you than Nigel Cobb.' So that put Dad's mind at rest and besides, Nigel had pointed out that the risk factor in moving me in an ambulance to London could be immense. The legs might not stand up, he felt, to travelling any distance. The operation had to be done right away.

Dad, still showing some concern over Nigel's credentials, asked him if he felt competent to do the kind of surgery that was required in this case. 'Have you ever done anything like this before? Can you do it?' he queried.

Someone with Nigel's professional expertise might well have told him to piss off, but he knew Dad was very worried about the situation and showed no sign of being offended by the question. Nigel promised Franco he would do the best he could, as he would do with any patient, but he was still unsure how bad the internal damage was. Dad finally accepted that I would be in extremely capable hands and I was wheeled out of the private ward to have what turned out to be an eight-hour operation involving the most complex surgery. As the orderlies pushed me towards the theatre, Dad shouted to Nigel, 'Ring me straight away if there is the slightest risk of you having to amputate. God knows how I will be able to tell Barry if that has to be the case. I know he'll never forgive me.'

Once the operation was over, Nigel phoned Dad to tell him the legs and the hand would be OK — and you must have been able to hear the sigh of relief all over Northamptonshire. That pressure on Dad was ridiculous and sometimes I wonder who was suffering most in all this.

Nigel Cobb described my shattered bones as being like crushed eggs. Upon opening up my legs, he was confronted by a confusion of bones, muscles and tendons on either side.

With powerful drugs minimising the risk of infection, Nigel and his team set to work, using the latest technology. Twenty-seven screws, made from space-age alloy with specially-grooved heads to prevent the bone growing over them, were put in, with two seven-inch long buttresses and a pair of five-inch plates made from Swiss steel pliable enough to be shaped by hand to suit the size of the bone. Inserting the buttresses and plates, which support the fragments of bone until they knit, presented some difficulty because the surgeons had to find pieces of bone big enough to accept a screw.

The pain, afterwards, gradually decreased. It wasn't leaving me writhing in agony, as some people might have thought. The drugs took care of that. My chief concern was the worry over what the future held. Would my body ever be normal? Would I be able to get on a bike OK? How stupid, I realised, when I reassessed the situation the following day. Everything was going to be just as it had been, I reassured myself. All I had got to do was to get my arse into gear and get back to what I was doing before this rude interruption.

Although I regard myself as a Christian and do believe in God, I didn't pray in hospital when there was some doubt over the future of my legs. I reckon He looked after me in the crash but I'm not such a hypocrite as to get on to the Guy only when I'm in need of outside help. I don't mind admitting I prayed for Niki Lauda and Didier Peroni when they had bad smashes but I don't do it any other time, so why should I contact Him only in moments of personal distress? God helps those who help themselves...and God help those caught helping themselves!

Afterwards, Nigel showed me the X-rays and explained, stage by stage, what he had done. He convinced me that my legs would eventually be as they were. The bones might even heal stronger. The same was true of the wrist — provided that I was prepared to work hard at the physiotherapy to get the joints and muscles back into shape. It was fantastic news — I even smiled for the first time. What a lot I had to be grateful for to Nigel and his team for their marathon stint on the operating table.

The right knee had broken cleanly below the knee and was therefore a fairly simple matter. But the left knee joint had disintegrated and that was the big problem when the time came to reshape it. The left leg, some might recall, was the one I damaged so badly at Daytona, which had subsequently needed a steel rod inserted to strengthen it. The two plates in each leg will be removed in about two years, as will the 26 screws inserted in the legs, together with another plate and five more screws in my wrist. In fact, Nigel had to remove a couple of old screws from a previous bang on the knee I did at Mallory in 1975.

Apart from some torn ligaments in the left shoulder, everything else remained intact, Oh, I did whack what I term my lusting tackle on the tank extremely hard. That really hurt! That part of my anatomy soon got better but I have to say the one enjoyment in life I did miss lying in a hospital bed was sex. Steph was with me nearly all the time but a hospital's not the easiest place in the world to get your leg over! It's pretty difficult getting up to mischief with nurses and doctors scurrying about, especially with the legs in the shape they were in. Though I shouldn't mention it in the same breath, being away from my helicopter was a wrench too. I would spend all day, every day flying it if I had the opportunity, I get so much pleasure from it.

Nigel answered me honestly and directly when I asked him if I would be all right to race again, the first question I put to him when I came from the operation. 'Yes, you'll be all right to race, without any doubt,' he replied.

'But what happens if I bang the legs again, perhaps in another crash?' I asked.

'Well,' he said, 'the metal inside is very thin and all that would happen is that the plates would to out of shape. It would on the face of it, be a straightforward case of replacing the metal.'

Fears have been expressed that my bones might be unable to take any further battering from more crashes; the prospect of one further tumble and what it would do to me should weigh pretty heavily on my mind, many people think. Let me say that after Daytona I rode for three years with the steel pin in my leg knowing that the rod would shatter my leg in a bad accident. That was in the back of my mind all the time, but it didn't make me ride any slower. If something is going to happen, it will happen. No-one can do anything about it. If I had been destined to die that day at Silverstone, I would have died. But clearly I wasn't meant to die — I survived to tell the tale. Yet who can say I won't be clobbered by a bus tomorrow? Or fall out of the sky from my helicopter? You just never know. Look at Mike Hailwood — all those years racing and never hurt himself, then loses his life in an ordinary road accident.

But had the Silverstone accident been my fault, had I been riding too fast or too hard, or taking a chance, which I never do, then I would certainly give serious thought to packing it in. But the calamity wasn't of my own making. I couldn't do anything about it. The same is true of my Daytona mishap. I wasn't forewarned that the rear tyre was going to blow out and the bike would spit me off. So what's the point in worrying that something bad is going to happen? If I was the sort of competitor who only won races by repeatedly taking chances, through riding beyond the limit, then I would be asking for trouble. But if something goes wrong, as happened at Silverstone, well, that's life. And I'm only too aware that rotten things can happen.

What caused me acute embarrassment after my Silverstone crash, were the national newspaper headlines like 'Brave

Barry' and crap like that. I didn't consider myself as brave. All I had to do was to get the legs mended as quickly as possible and get back on a bike. What's brave about that?

When I was out on the track that July afternoon, I was not anticipating an accident. But our lads in the Falklands, for instance, were well aware of the dangers they were facing and some might have thought they could be having their last day of life on earth. That's what I call being brave, not lying in a hospital bed waiting to get better after coming to grief doing something enjoyable. Guys injured in the Falklands conflict could well be confined to a wheelchair for the rest of their lives. But I'll be photographed walking on crutches coming out of a restaurant and the newspaper headlines will label me as being brave. Priorities can so often be confused.

There's nothing brave about attempting to ride a motorcycle again. But it's brave when you see your mate next to you blown up, or charge over a hill knowing the same fate might await you.

I was told I'd be in hospital for eight weeks but the signs were encouraging when after two weeks I was fully bending the right leg and half-bending the other.

Betsy Newton, my physio, would give me daily instructions: 'Bend this that way, get that further round there,' and so on. At night instead of falling asleep I got into the habit of working on the exercise movements she had drummed into me and so when she called in each morning, I'd impress her with my improving leg movements. Staying awake at night like that, though, left me dog-tired in the daytime!

By then, I'd moved out of the general hospital to a private nursing home, the Three Shires, a mile away, which had been recommended to me. However, I was fed up being in hospitals and made up my mind I wanted to get back to my home at Charlwood. Although the staff and the treatment were first class, I was sure my rehabilitation would go better in surroundings in which I felt happier. (Incidentally I paid the medical bills, not Yamaha). Nigel agreed to my release, knowing I would not relax my physiotherapy programme because of my burning desire to be one hundred percent fit again as quickly as possible.

The loss of my independence, I suppose, was my biggest handicap: not being able to go where I wanted without seeking assistance from someone willing to drag me about.

For the first week, I had no desire to eat anything and, consequently, as my body had to live off something, my muscles began to reduce. My chest is normally 42½. When I left hospital, it was down to 38. All my tee-shirts and sweaters suddenly appeared baggy on me. I lost an incredible three inches around the base of my right arm. But for all that shrivelling, I had only gone down 12 pounds, to 9 stone.

What perked me up no end was the mountain of get-well cards and telegrams, around 25,000, from all sorts of people and from all over the world. There must have been 10,000 cards from abroad. It was a sign that a lot of people cared about my well-being and I must say it felt good to know there was a lot of sympathy for my misfortune.

My girlfriend Steph had spent every day at my bedside, keeping my spirits up during those early, painful weeks and caring for my every need. Once I dozed off she would leave to stay the night at Lord Hesketh's house at Easton Neston and would be back at breakfast time. My parents were allowed to park their caravan in the hospital car park so they could keep a close vigil in the difficult, trying period.

I tried to receive as many visitors as I could, and there seemed to be a constant stream entering the room, quite a few of them press men who tried to wring every conceivable story out of me. As I was earning no wages and had little prospect of doing so for some time, I had to do a financial deal with one Fleet Street daily for an exclusive.

The press treatment of my Silverstone accident was, on the whole, fair. The only exception was an article in the *Mail on Sunday* which I considered to be most uncomplimentary. The theme of the story suggested I was a complete idiot to talk about wanting to return to racing. When I came out of the Three Shires nursing home with what looked like half of Fleet Street there to greet me, I shouted out to a pushing, heaving press corps, 'Is there anyone here from the *Mail on Sunday*?'

'Well, I'm from the *Daily Mail* but I assure you it wasn't me who wrote that story. I know it must have upset you,' a bloke answered.

Had I buttonholed the person in question, he would have had the chance to hear some frank comments, which might not have been suitable for publication in a family newspaper!

I had half expected to see one or two officials from Silverstone circuit while I was still in hospital but, like the flag marshals at Abbey Curve, they were nowhere to be seen. If they had come in just to say hello, I certainly wouldn't have ignored them. Still, I didn't give a monkey's.

After my accident, a certain Silverstone employee was heard to say, I'm told, 'Christ, I wonder how many people we are going to lose through the gate.'

Vernon Cooper, Chairman of the Road Race Committee of the Auto-Cycle Union, the governing motorcycling sports body in Britain, was another who failed to make an appearance, although I didn't think he would make an effort anyway. Up until a few years ago, I was paid a fee by Silverstone, for undertaking PR work for the British Grand Prix to promote the event, but I think the ACU was instrumental in stopping that, believing people would go to the meeting regardless of whether or not I was riding.

All I will say is that we don't get on together and the ACU would appear to stand for the Auto-Cooper Union.

As I've always maintained, it's us, the riders, who can pay the ultimate price with the sacrifice of our lives. We deserve to have as leader of our sport someone with balanced views and one who can appreciate the rider's viewpoint.

Cooper has also claimed that I want the British GP switched from its Silverstone home to Donington Park. I feel the organisers at Donington have put a lot into motorcycle racing and have the right attitude towards riders and safety. They deserve to have a crack at staging the British Grand Prix. Donington have at least five major meetings every season. Silverstone run so few events each year. Why should they have a monpoly of the biggest money-spinner of the lot?

As a circuit, there is little wrong with Silverstone. But I regard Donington Park as a more deserving track. The people behind Donington have made an effort over the last few years to make motorcycling work and have invested a lot of money into two wheels. But what have they done at Silverstone, apart from creaming off the Grand Prix and running some minor clubman's race? When motorcycling meetings are run at Donington, the marshals are genuine bikers. That's not always the case at Silverstone which, in all honesty, has to be regarded as a car circuit, with car-orientated people running the place.

I know there has been some criticism of the Donington track surface, which does seem slippery. A heavy cloudburst too can present problems at Donington with moisture remaining in the crevices of the tarmacadam and seemingly taking ages to dry out. But once you've done a couple of laps, you're completely aware it is slippery and you're prepared for it. It's the same for everyone and as long as everyone rides within the capabilities of their tyres, there should be no difficulty in getting round safely. If all the top riders considered the Donington track conditions too tricky to handle, they would not turn up there every year for the big internationals.

At the time of the accident, I commented angrily on the practice-day set-up at Silverstone — a day when the ACU had no involvement — and I stand by my words. I regret nothing I have said because they expressed feelings that I honestly believe to be right. Once upon a time, perhaps, my remarks on certain issues have upset people and landed me in trouble. But now I stand by what I say.

With my medical bills and loss of earnings amounting to somewhere in the region of £300,000, I threatened to sue the owners of Silverstone over the crash. Their callous attitude toward my accident annoyed me but the essence of my legal action would have to lie in the track's marshals on the day of question.

Had I known they couldn't afford to field an adequate number of marshals, I would have organised a whip-round. With more marshals present on the day, I'm sure I wouldn't have had my accident.

But I need no reminding that I'll be forced to return to that track if, as is most likely, the British Grand Prix is staged there again in the future. My feelings won't change, though, and it doesn't mean that I have to say nice things about them.

The sad fact is that I have enjoyed racing at Silverstone. I like it as a race track and it has got to be regarded as a safe circuit under proper racing conditions. I think it's a great circuit to race on.

There's no grudge against the track — just the people who organise the place and are responsible for the marshals. Those are who I blame.

3
AFTERMATH

1982 had been a financially disastrous year and my position wasn't helped when I heard that John Player was planning to withdraw its support from my team at the end of the season.

I guess someone at the top of Player preferred Formula One racing to motorcycles, regarding it as a wise move to pump any spare money into the Lotus team. As far as column inches were concerned, however, I grabbed more editorial space in the first two weeks of racing in '82 than Team Lotus did in the whole year. My cuttings library supplies the evidence.

Some might have thought that the considerable publicity my crash generated would enhance my professional standing, for more people would be aware of my existence and the risks we riders have to face. But I was anxious we should not milk the accident simply for the publicity as it would tend to give motorcycling a bad name, supporting the idea that two wheels are bad news, if not downright dangerous. In one of the first interviews I gave in hospital, I spelt it out clearly: I didn't want outsiders to believe that motorcyclists were just a bunch of brainless thickos. I certainly don't think I am one.

Rather than having my name splashed over the front page of the dailies for a crash, I would be happier getting some column inches of coverage on the sports page, from which the punters can draw a clearer understanding and appreciation of bike racing.

My departure from the hospital was shown on all the television channels and a lot of people commented to me afterwards about how well I looked so soon after the accident. But I'm no different from the next patient; I possess no special healing qualities. I just believe getting better starts with the mind. You must make yourself believe your recovery will be swift and positive. The body won't co-operate unless the mind is in the right attitude.

As soon as I arrived home at Charlwood, I set about my training programme. The pain-killers were no longer needed in the daytime but the discomfort at night meant I had to give myself an injection in the backside each evening. I must tell you; it's one thing having a nurse stick it in you, it's another thing altogether doing it yourself.

Once I overcame the pain barrier, a couple of weeks after the actual crash, I began to realise that these moments of sheer agony were becoming all too regular. I don't look forward to the next time, if there is a next time, when something else goes wrong. The prospect of having my body, no matter which part, wracked with pain, scares me. I've endured enough in my racing career and the thought of more physical punishment coming my way sends shivers of fear through my body. My toes curl with terror when I even contemplate a visit to the dentist: the injection, the drill...Then there was the suffering from a somewhat straight-forward operation to scrape my sinuses which frequently cause me trouble. The anguish those needles gave me, poked high up my nostrils, was sheer hell. I hated it. The staff were genuinely surprised to hear me worrying about the impending excruciating tor-ture. They considered this operation was small beer alongside what had happened to me in the past.

With regular sessions on a stationary exercise bike and some muscle-building tackle I put together from bits out of the workshop, I was quickly becoming semi-mobile again, although the pace was slow and I could only make short journeys.

The hamstrings and the muscles at the back of the legs were the first priority and I'd go to one of the plush hotels near Gatwick Airport where they had a small indoor swimming pool. Steph would take me to the poolside in the wheel chair and I'd slide into the water. After a few days, I encountered few problems with swimming. With vigorous kicking I found I was getting more and more bend back in my knees.

Despite the strenuous physiotherapy programme I had

mapped out and kept to rigidly, there was one nagging
doubt. No matter how confident I felt about my return to
complete fitness, the works team and prospective backers
might just wonder if I would be in tip-top shape in time for
the new season. Would I be riding as hard in the future? I
knew perfectly well I would be as strong as before and that
my will to win would not have diminished. But the world had
to be shown that recovery was going to be swift and complete
and any idea that I might not be the same kind of rider on the
track needed to be immediately dispelled.

The muscles and ligaments, slowly, but surely, began to
sort themselves out and the bones were knitting into the right
patterns. Within a few weeks of leaving hospital I had 135
degrees of movement in both knees. Three months after the
Silverstone smash, I had total articulation of the broken left
wrist and the legs had become strong enough to require just
one walking stick as a precautionary support. My recovery
was moving apace! I'm convinced my history of rapid
healings is the result of eating good food full of the right
nutritional ingredients.

What really knocked me out was the reception everyone
—crowd and officials—gave me when I brought the
helicopter into Donington Park. I had previously told
Donington's circuit owner Tom Wheatcroft that with two
broken legs and a broken wrist it was a slow and painful
struggle learning to walk again with the aid of crutches.
Jokingly I said I could probably ride a motorbike easier than I
could walk. That put their minds into overtime and they
immediately thought of what was unthinkable eight weeks
before: me taking out a bike. And all I had intended was to
have a day out to see all the lads in the paddock again! I
certainly hadn't meant to do anything more than watch a bit
of racing. But things developed quickly as Donington Park
recognised the fact that 20,000 customers might like to have a
look at me.

They asked me if I would to round the track in a roadster
and I knew it would be no great hardship. I had built up sufficient strength to handle a machine in those circumstances.

I got onto Nigel Cobb immediately to ensure he was put in the picture as to what I was planning. After all he had done for me, I wanted to be confident I got his blessing. But I warned him the newspapers might try to blow up my return to the track out of all proportion, and suggested they would manufacture headlines like 'Sheene rides against doctor's orders', or 'Sheene defies surgeon'.

Nigel had to fend off endless calls from writers looking for that angle and resolutely refused to say whether he considered there was any risk factor. Both he and I knew what we were doing, and the intention was to ensure there would be no dodgy moments. He knew I wouldn't land myself in trouble and I certainly didn't contemplate aggravating any of my injuries. The only people unhappy were the Fleet Street boys who could not obtain the kind of story they so desperately wanted.

I had Steve Parrish on the pillion seat of the Yamaha, but only in case the engine stalled. If the bike had stopped for some reason, I would have toppled over like something out of a Monty Python sketch and I wasn't prepared to take that risk. Steve expressed some worries afterwards because we were hitting ninety down the straight but I was too busy talking to him to check the dials.

To be truthful, I wasn't greatly bothered about getting my leg over a bike again. I got much more pleasure flying the helicopter up to Donington. I had noticed to my horror on the bottom of my helicopter pilot's licence, that if you are incapacitated for more than twenty days you have to undertake another medical examination. Not only that, but my medical certificate had expired the week after my crash. When the civil aviation doctor at Gatwick saw me cruise into his surgery in a wheelchair, he couldn't believe I was going to pass the test. He obviously wouldn't even consider issuing the certificate with me in the wheelchair. But when a few weeks later I was up and about on crutches and he had consulted Nigel Cobb about my condition, all was well. If I couldn't fly a helicopter again, I would be devastated. I intend to fly helicopters for many years after I've given up racing. If there was any money in the aviation world that I could earn, that's what I'd do when I quit racing. Unfortunately, there's no money in flying.

Being off work proved costly. From a financial point of view, the meetings I missed from August through to the end of the season denied me the chance to pick up at least £150,000. Besides lucrative international events on the Continent, there were races at Donington, Brands Hatch, and in Japan and Malaya where I could have earned excellent money both for starting and for doing well.

But there I was, almost unemployed, with not a penny coming into the house since July and with all my overheads to take care of. Mechanics' wages alone amounted to almost £500 a week. But as there was nothing for them to work on, I had to let them go. None of us were immune from the recession! Fortunately Ken Fletcher, my Kiwi main spannerman, had been offered a ridiculous amount of money to live and work in France for Sonauto, the French Yamaha importers, the sort of offer I just was unable to match. Luckily I have been able to tempt him back. Another one, Simon, was found a job with Mitsui. But he'll be back with me for the 1983 campaign and so will Robert the Daf transporter driver.

Looming up was the annual round of discussion over bikes and sponsorship for the following year which becomes more and more of a headache for everyone involved in this sport. The bargaining position a world championship gives you in terms of securing the best contractual deals and the top bikes for the following year is immense. It should be the passport to riches. Even if I couldn't quite have managed top place in 1982, I reckoned coming runner-up was on the cards, which might have strengthened my claim when seeking sponsors. Still, coming equal fourth only 8 points behind Crosby after missing four rounds and breaking down in others, was reasonable going I thought.

Silverstone has never been a happy hunting ground—I have crashed at Silverstone twice before at high speed. The first time was way back in 1973 when I was tyre testing in mid-week for Dunlop who had booked the circuit. As I was going through Club Corner on my 750cc three-cylinder Suzuki, on a perfect day, the front end went away and the bike and I slid along the road towards Abbey Curve. The bike must have been doing at least 120 mph but I just couldn't make out why this should happen for no apparent reason.

The bike burst into flames and the palms of my hands were severly burned. By the time I had been patched up, and the tyre technicians had examined every possible cause, Dunlop's Dave Buck cleared up the mystery: the crash was caused by a fat garden earthworm wriggling across the tarmac. At the point where the front wheel slid away were the two halves of the juicy worm with the middle section completely flattened where I had run over it. With the bike angled over, the moist slippery innards of the squashed worm took away any contact between the rubber and road and down we went. It all sounds too ridiculous for words but the tyre mark over the worm was there for all to see. Worst thing about that episode was that the bike was almost a complete write-off and had to be rebuilt in just three days for the next crucial Superbike Championship round at Brands Hatch.

Then, of course there was the '81 British Grand Prix tumble on the second lap of the 500cc race. We were coming down Hangar Straight and the plan was to sit behind the leaders for three-quarters of the race and then go for it. But everyone appeared to be riding so slowly. Bugger this, I thought, I'm going to clear off. As I braked early going into Stowe Corner, I reckoned that was the time to take the lead. I got the power on early and really got a run on Crosby. But just as I was on the point of taking him, his Suzuki slid sideways to the left and then appeared to go straight on. There was no possibility of getting through on either side. It seemed as if it was a straight choice of running into Crosby or his bike. Well, I couldn't hit him whatever I might do to myself and so I slammed the front disc brakes on while I was cranked over, which pushed the front end out. Off I went into the catch fencing, finishing not far from Crosby. I escaped with a broken bone in my heel and a broken finger, which stopped any chances of continuing the race. I didn't even bother inspecting the bike for damage. What was the point? It looked in a sorry state at first glance and I was in no condition to carry on this time. Had I been OK, I might well have sprinted over to the machine and whacked the handlebars with my fist. Checking for breaks in the bars is always my first move if a bike falls down; then a quick check of the brakes to make sure they are still functioning: anything else that might have gone wrong you can just about cope with. But this time the bike was wrecked, I was feeling somewhat sore, and that was the end of the race for me.

It was just the luck of the draw. It was the sort of incident that can happen in racing. I was reported as being seething with anger with Crosby for causing the accident that denied me an outside chance of winning the title. But I wasn't angry with him; my annoyance was directed against the specialist press who could not appreciate precisely what I had to do to avoid running him over.

The press started by winding Crosby up and seemed to think that because Roberts, who was behind me, managed to get through I should have been able to as well. But the press boys didn't realise that I had no option but to grab a fistful of brake, while Kenny was in a position where he could get through unhindered. Had Crosby's bike not changed direction when it was out of control, I could well have been unimpeded and it would have been Kenny who would have copped it.

The press were trying to make something out of nothing. Contrary to what first appeared in print in *Motor Cycle News*, Croz and I were speaking afterwards. The problem was that both of us had our own columns in the same paper and the editor at the time felt, mistakenly, that it would be a good idea to let Crosby have a go at me with the intention of getting me wound up, playing one rider off against the other. Perhaps instead of attempting to develop what the public might have considered to be a personal feud, they should have looked more closely into why the highly-developed tyre on Crosby's Yamaha gave way and consequently ruined the race. That would have made far more interesting, informative reading.

I had a column in *Motor Cycle News* for many years,

which gave an insight into what life is really like at the top level of racing. After each weekend I would discuss several topics with whoever happened to be the road-racing reporter on the paper at the time. But my patience eventually ran out with this journal when it began to publish stories about me which were a long way from being accurate. There was one crazy story in *MCN* about me, riding for Yamaha at the time, being seen at Heron Suzuki's headquarters in Beddington Lane, Croydon, where I was supposed to be having talks with them about bikes. This piece was published in *MCN* in a summertime issue in 1981. No-one had bothered to get hold of me to discover the facts. Yes, I had gone to Suzuki's place ... six months previously, to complete the payments on a machine bought by my friend Roberto Pietri. Meeting former colleagues again like Peter Agg and Maurice Knight gave us a chance to talk about the old times. But not one word was mentioned about my riding for them. As I was happily set up with Yamaha, there was no reason for the subject to come up. I just couldn't understand how such an inaccurate story could get into the paper. I also felt that the paper had began to show a bias against me, for no reason that I could ever establish. The then editor definitely had a chip on his shoulder: pure sensationalism was one thing, incorrect factual information quite another. So it reached the point where I said to the editor I was unhappy with the relationship, and I swapped my allegiance to the other weekly paper, *Motor Cycle Weekly*. Not, I should add, that I've severed all relations. I still answer questions from *MCN* reporters. The latest editor has tried to clear up much of the ill-feeling that built up and I co-operate with his boys as much as possible. Besides, I still enjoy attending their 'Man of the Year' presentations, particularly if the readers have voted me into top place. If you know the readers of the biggest-selling motorcycling paper in the world are behind you, things can't be too bad.

I well remember the 1979 function at London's Lyceum, that historic dance hall just off the Strand. I was still officially a Suzuki GB rider at the time but it was common knowledge that I was all set to race for Yamaha the following year, ending an association that had lasted seven good years. So when the awards were made, in reverse order, culminating with me being called on stage to receive the 'Man of the Year' trophy, I was wearing a Yamaha jumper.

People said afterwards it went down like a lead balloon with the Suzuki chiefs seated in the balcony, who may have felt the title was earned from results achieved riding their machines. I wore the jumper for a bit of fun, just to aggravate race chief Maurice Knight who, to his credit, took it in good part. All that happened was that Suzuki stopped the last payment due to me under the terms of my annual contract but I knew when I pulled the stunt that I would forfeit the pay cheque. I suggested that the cheque in question went to the Joan Seeley Pain Relief Fund but I never established if that happened. I had by then largely severed my ties with Suzuki, and the wearing of the special jumper with the Yamaha logo displayed on the front, was a goodwill gesture to my new employers.

Sometimes I think of what might have happened in '82 if I had been given the V-4 sooner. It has been suggested that Crosby had first bite ahead of me because the bike had a left-hand gear change, while I prefer a right-hand gear shift, and nearly every racing bike I've been on has had it on that side. Fifteen years ago when I started, all bikes were built with the lever on the right. The shift to the left-hand gear change was made primarily for the American market where they are used to left-hand drive and I'm not sure I want to ride a bike with the gear shift in the unorthodox position. The only time I was involved with unorthodox gears was back in '71 in the Czechoslovakian Grand Prix, when I was hired to race a 50cc Kriedler. It went one gear down, five up, which was the reverse of my normal pattern and as it was on the left as well, it put me in all kinds of bother. This was my first experience of a fifty and it seemed a miniscule machine after what I had been used to. Howling into the first corner I completely forgot the gearing arrangement and almost high-sided it. But a few laps later I began to get the hang of it and I went on to win the race. That victory in the tiddler class leaves me with the record of being the only racer to have won 50, 125, and

500cc Grands Prix but I can't consider that to be any special achievement.

In any case, these days the factory would have little difficulty in moving the gear change to whichever side suited the rider; and if that is Yamaha's reason for allowing Crosby to test the V-4 before me, it is a most flimsy one.

However trivial a matter one may consider that test session to be, the fact remains that had I been given an earlier opportunity to get to grips with the machine, instead of having to rush everything in a few short days, the Silverstone episode might not have occurred. No matter how apparently unimportant, that move might, and I emphasise might, have had a bearing on the disastrous events that were to follow.

Meanwhile my absence from the tracks, and any doubts the public might feel about my ability to return to total fitness, did not bother me. As my injuries improved week by week, there was no reason at all why a prospective sponsor should shy away from me. I knew I would soon be on the tracks as good as new, ready and willing to compete as strongly as ever. The only obstacle in my way was the world recession which makes it so much harder now to encourage a backer to invest in the sport than was the case five years ago. Everyone is suffering, in all forms of motorsport, from the top right down to the bottom.

But I knew for a fact that whoever put their money behind me and my team would get blanket coverage whenever I rode. After all the fuss the press made about my leaving hospital and then riding the roadster at Donington, it was patently obvious that my return to the race circuit would command an awful lot of attention, on a world-wide scale. Win, draw or lose, the sponsors would get their advertising coverage, which is the whole point of getting involved with any sport. How many other sportsmen could offer that attraction?

But there was no possibility of making the crash and my survival the big sales pitch in my search for fresh sponsors. I wanted them to support me quite simply as a racer with the best possible chance to restore British pride on the race tracks of the world. I didn't want a massive hue and cry about the comeback; all I required was the right sponsor to run my racing team.

4
BEGINNINGS

My school days were the most miserable of my life. I detested school. The lessons were boring and the teachers, given the thankless task of drilling some knowledge into me, always appeared intent on showing me up in front of my class-mates.

It wasn't that I couldn't handle the work: in my heart I knew I could hold my own against the other pupils. But I adopted a policy of non-cooperation. I felt I wanted to be the school rebel, and I resisted all the coaxing and cajoling of the teachers at both junior and, after failing my 11-plus exam, secondary modern schools, in central London.

It was the teachers' attitude that riled me most and brought out the streak of defiance that has remained with me ever since. Their methods were domineering and uncompromising, involving regular canings each term, and discouraged me from wanting to get to grips with my education.

But slices of luck did come my way. One typical day at St. Martin-in-the-fields school, during a break between lessons, I was spotted fighting in the playground by a lady peering over the wall. 'Do you like fighting?' she asked. I replied that if you didn't know how to fight you would get trampled on. Then she enquired if I could sing, and I said I perhaps could, if pressed.

She was recruiting lads as extras for the opera *Tosca* at Covent Garden, just around the corner, and another young boy and I were auditioned and given small parts in the first act to scrap in a churchyard scene. Cast as a singing, fighting hooligan wasn't altogether at odds with the way I behaved in real life! Sharing the stage with Tito Gobbi and Maria Callas at such a famous place became one of my most vivid childhood memories. I even had to sing! Best part of it was it meant getting off school.

I have always retained an interest in music, although I've no over-riding passion for classical opera. My musical tastes basically revolve around middle-of-the-road pop and when much later I was invited by Roy Plomley to appear on BBC Radio Four's Desert Island Discs my choice of records reflected that taste. Still favourites with me, the records I selected were: *San Jose* by Dionne Warwick; *Crackerbox Palace* by George Harrison; *New Kid in Town* by The Eagles; *Don't let the Sun Catch You Crying* by Jose Feliciano; *Nights on Broadway* by Candi Staton; *In the Mood* by Glen Miller; *Sunshine after the Rain* by Elkie Brooks; and *If you Leave me Now* by Chicago.

Once free of the shackles of school, I wanted to prove I was bright and possessed some kind of ability. I've always been really determined. At school I resolved I was not going to let the teachers feel they had got the better of me, and I stuck to it. I had quickly slipped from the A stream down to the C stream. But one year, with exams approaching, I decided to make a very late effort to give everyone a shock. I finished third in the class and left the teachers amazed that I could have made such a vast improvement in such a short period of time.

But still I left school without a single qualification, apart from the unenviable achievement of having topped the absenteeism record. Only the metalwork teacher gave me any encouragement. Recognising my enthusiasm for the subject, he gave me a free hand with the tools and materials and I was constantly top of the form in metalwork.

Even though I was troubled with asthma as a boy, I rarely considered the health hazards connected with smoking. At school I was constantly in trouble for smoking—I started when I was nine—and even now I normally get through 40 untipped Gitanes each day, and try to ignore the dangers which I know exist. But, of course, lots of things in life can be harmful—like racing motorbikes!

My asthmatic condition ruled me out of active sports at school even though I was soundly built. It made regular

breathing difficult whenever I began to run, although it did
not prevent me from swimming, which is about the only
sport I've had the inclination to take up. Physical contact
games like football and rugby never appealed to me and,
whereas many of my school chums would discuss endlessly
the merits of soccer stars at the time, I much preferred to involve myself in tinkering with engines.

Once an asthma attack — and there were many — hit me
while I was watching the Isle of Man TT races. As a family
we would go there most years, with my father assisting with
the preparation of a rider's bike. When I was about five, I had
to be rushed to Noble's Hospital in Douglas after a doctor
had been called to attend a bad attack. I was kept in for three
days until my breathing returned to normal and it was safe
for me to go home.

Gradually, however, the respiration trouble disappeared in
my early teens, and I realised that I would no longer be able
to use the excuse to my teachers that I was away from school
through attending the local asthma clinic. Something had to
be done. My medical problem was known to the teachers,
who understood when I produced a doctor's appointment
card every week showing I had to be examined at 10.15 am
on a Wednesday, followed by a visit to the bronchitis clinic
at 2.15 pm. But what I had done was to pick up a mass of
blank appointment cards on a previous, legitimate visit and
to encourage a mate's father to fill in the details, signing a fic-
titious doctor's signature. That way my handwriting
wouldn't be identified.

This left me free to stay away from school and I'd often go
down to Brands Hatch race circuit in Kent intent on watching
the mid-week practice sessions or, if I was lucky, I might be
asked to work on a guy's bike.

From the earliest opportunity, my father Frank had been
keen to have me alongside him in the workshop at the back of
our flat in Holborn. He would demonstrate, when time permitted, the correct way to strip and rebuild motorcycle
engines. This kind of learning was fun! Encouraged to meddle
with the various parts of any machine in for repair or
modification, I soon began to pick up little bits of basic

knowledge and such an early start no doubt laid the foundations later in life for an understanding of mechanical matters.

Once a useful club racer, Dad established a reputation in our part of London as a tuner, and as soon as he finished his daily routine as a general maintenance man at the Royal College of Surgeons — where my mother Iris also was employed as a housekeeper — a steady stream of enthusiasts would bring their motorbikes to Dad, confident he would breathe new life into them.

He would pay for trips to the Isle of Man, and to Spain where we would combine a holiday with a visit to the Bultaco factory, a marque Dad had been connected with over a number of years. It was Dad's Spanish link that led to us calling him Franco, a nickname that has stuck with him, one he never objects to.

Growing up in a motorcycle-dominated atmosphere naturally had some bearing on where my future might lie, although it has to be said that Dad did not push me into a life of bikes in a bid to achieve glories that had eluded him.

By all accounts, I had a penchant for speed as a toddler, first on a tricycle in the backyard and then on a 50cc four-stroke Ducati, rebuilt by Dad. At the age of 5, every spare moment was spent on that two-speed bike, much to the annoyance of the neighbours, who regularly complained to the police about the noise. I quickly mastered throttle and brake operation but tended to by-pass the clutch. The bike was capable of speeds not far short of 50 mph, but my parents felt I was safer pottering in my own yard than risking life and limb playing near the traffic of the busy London streets.

The next step was to graduate to cars. Dad had doctored the pedals of a battered Austin 10, which had cost him £5, for my short eight-year-old legs, and I would take school friends on racing laps of the yard, even teaching my sister Margaret — five years my senior and now married to former racer Paul Smart — to drive it.

When Dad came to an arrangement with Bultaco to import their new racers, he would allow me to ride them on disused airfields in order to run them in before they went to custo-

mers. Then there would be times when I gingerly took out
racing machines he had hotted up, to check that everything
was functioning properly. Being only eleven at the time, I
was clearly being presented with the chance to explore the
idiosyncracies of a variety of motorbikes at an age when
other kids were struggling just to repair push bikes.

Dad and I would be at motorcycle race meetings most
weekends from March to October, partly for his freelance
tuning work but mostly for the pleasure that both of us found
as spectators. For riding around the paddocks I had first a
Triumph Tiger Cub and then a Bultaco Sherpa, which enabled me to become proficient in controlling a bike over rough
ground.

On occasions, stretching my luck, I'd ride the machines
round our neighbourhood, only to be caught by our friendly
bobby who would let me off with a tongue-lashing. The fact
that Dad did some private work on the cheap for the local
force may have helped the police to overlook my illegalities!

Little by little, I was building a useful store of information
on how bikes operated. I would watch trained mechanics in
the pits fiddle with engines, ask a stream of involved questions and observe from the trackside how different bikes Dad
had prepared performed when ridden by different riders.
Looking and listening in my early teens was to pay rich
dividends in years to come.

Not all my time, though, was spent in my father's company. As a growing lad, I began to take more than a passing
interest in girls and Saturday nights would see me and my
pals heading for the Empire ballroom in Leicester Square.
From the time I was fourteen, I could dance well, and that
was the best way to pick up ladies in those days. It is fairly
common knowledge now that I lost my virginity over a
snooker table, thanks to a pretty girl whose name is lost in
the mist of time — as are so many of them now.

While I was a rebel at school, I tended to be obedient at
home, and this firm, stable family relationship has acted as
a wonderful calming influence throughout my career. My
parents are invariably with me at race meetings and it's nice
to know they can still get excited about seeing me race.

On reflection, I suppose I displayed two different characters, refusing to conform to the educational rules on one
hand, and being as pleasant and helpful as I could to Frank
and Iris on the other. Whereas I found great difficulty in having to address a schoolmaster as 'sir', I tried to be as polite as
possible to my parents, perhaps because of their willingness
to allow me the freedom of expression denied me by the
school system. My parents treated me as an adult, but even
so I was amazed when they raised no objections to my going
to the Continent for a short spell to work as a Grand Prix
mechanic. And I was only 14!

I was really delighted when Tony Woodman, an American
friend of the family, asked me to go with him to help with his
bikes at Grands Prix in Austria and West Germany; astound-
ed really, because he obviously had such confidence in my
mechanical ability.

This was an opportunity to spread my wings and to get
away from my mother's cries of 'Barry, don't go outside without your jacket — remember your asthma'. Suddenly I was
on my own, with the horrible realisation that no parental
assistance would be forthcoming if I found myself puffing
and wheezing by the hour in the rear of a freezing van.

The whole expedition was a most satisfying experience and
at the time those few weeks spent in the company of the
world's greatest riders began to make me realise what fun it
could be to be involved with racing motorcycles as a full-time
occupation. I wasn't being paid by Tony, and didn't expect to
be. After all, it was more or less a working holiday. Dad had
tucked £15 into my pocket to tide me over the month away
from home but, as I wanted to spend every moment on working on Tony's G50 Matchless and 7R AJS, I came back to
London with change.

My parents had drafted a letter explaining the month's
leave of absence from school, and blaming my chest complaint. The headmaster never investigated. I suspect he was
relieved to have me out of circulation for four weeks, such
was my unruly behaviour.

Job prospects, or certainly the possibility of landing a job
that would stimulate my mind and still pay good money,

seemed bleak. Settling down to a career never occurred to me. When I left school, all I wanted to do was to race bikes at the weekend and work during the other five days to raise enough cash to support my effort.

My first position was in a Ford depot, placing spare parts in the right containers, the sheer monotony only relieved by the workshop radio beating out pop music. As that only paid a fiver a week, I looked for more lucrative employment. Acting as a motorcycle courier for a London advertising agency paid only a little more but it had its compensations — there was a BSA Bantam to hare around town on and it presented golden opportunities to chat up pretty receptionists and secretaries.

After Dad rebored that company bike, I fancy it was the fastest Bantam in London, and I always preferred it to my own 75cc Derbi which I was then riding on the public roads.

Then I landed a job valeting secondhand cars at a Central London garage and stuck that out for eighteen months. But the trickiest situation I ever got into was the time I went after work as a lorry driver. I showed my Dad's driving licence, which contained the required HGV stamp, and got over the age difficulty — I was eighteen but I said I was twenty-one. The manager agreed to take me on for a trial period and said I could take the vehicle home that night, ready for the first run the next morning. The loads were mostly antique furniture used as theatrical props in sets for television plays like *The Forsyte Saga*, which had to be delivered to the studios. I walked out to the compound and there stood a huge articulated lorry. My new boss shouted, 'Jump in — and give us a lift down the road, will you?'

Never having driven a lorry before, I had to act quickly to prevent him knowing I had absolutely no experience of handling a vehicle of this size and type.

'Look,' I said, 'I don't know who has been driving this thing but I want to be sure everything is OK and that it's roadworthy. I shall want to check through the vehicle's log and records so that I'm happy everything is OK.' I told him it could take me two hours to carry out the check and, impressed by my attitude, he went off, leaving me to try to distinguish one control from another.

Half an hour later, after discovering how to work the air brakes, I took it to the nearby car park where, for three hours, I familiarised myself with the behaviour of an 'artic' when driven forwards and backwards. Once I got the hang of it, I found it child's play, and the boss happily took me on the payroll after the successful month's trial. With that daytime work, and a night job parking cars in a multi-storey park at Olympia until two in the morning, I found I was able to build up my finances.

(In the late sixties, I humped round timber in a woodyard, to get together some extra cash to pay for a set of tyres, just another in a succession of somewhat unpredictable jobs of a manual nature.)

But after getting through my driving test at seventeen, I had enough money to run a Ford Thames van which my father supplied and I lost interest in riding a motorbike as a means of transport. Women, I quickly discovered, much preferred four wheels to two when it came to what you might loosely term 'courting'.

Thinking back to my first race, in 1968, in which I suffered the indignity of being hurled off, I sometimes wonder whether the sport was trying to tell me something. When the engine of Dad's 125cc Bultaco seized as I was lying second going into Kidney Bend at Brands Hatch I wondered what had hit me. Straight over the bars I went and walloped the tarmac with a resounding thwack — an experience that was to prove not uncommon in the years that lay ahead. Instead of climbing out of the ambulance dusting myself down and preparing for the second of my Dad's two races, perhaps I should have taken heed of the initial warning and, realising the dangers that could trap the unwary, settled for a less dangerous occupation.

But no, the seizure was a common weakness with two-stroke racing engines, and one should ride half in anticipation that something untoward might happen. Far from being turned off, I banished the unfortunate baptism from my mind, and I took third place in the second outing.

I can't say I live in fear of crashing. Like all riders at the highest level, I try to reduce the risk factor to an absolute minimum. But everyone makes mistakes, and teams of mechanics are no exception. The classic cock-up has to be in the Dutch TT at Assen in '81 when Kenny Roberts' men put on a wheel with a wet-weather tyre just before the start of the 500cc event. As Kenny returned to the grid after his warm-up lap, and halted his bike on the start-line, he was unable to rock the Yamaha — the front brake was jammed. In his haste to switch wheels, the Yamaha spannerman had inserted the brake pad back to front and, with the steel backing plate rubbing onto the disk, the pad had welded itself on. That was the GP, of course, in which Yamaha had a complete blow-out with Kenny sidelined right from the start, and I proved unable to coax my machine into life. It did splutter momentarily, after I had pushed it 200 yards, but weak carburation, the cause of the trouble, quickly silenced it.

But to return to my racing debut, I can recall being most gratified by what I had achieved so far and was suitably encouraged — as was Dad — to try another meeting the next weekend at Brands. It seemed like a good way to spend an afternoon. There was nothing cut-throat about the competition — just a bunch of enthusiastic guys in black leathers and pudding-basin helmets having a bit of fun.

When I managed to win both races at that second meeting, the thought never struck me that I had the necessary ability to make a mark in the sport. The fact that I elected early that same year to accompany abroad an international licence holder, Lewis Young, who was planning to do a season of world championships, indicated that I was not completely sold on the idea of actually being a racer myself. It was as if I wanted to complete my paddock apprenticeship by serving a final period as a hard-up over-worked mechanic.

Lewis was equipped with new 125cc and 250cc Bultacos, which was fortunate because it was the machine I knew most about and I could set up a bike with great confidence. We went from one Grand Prix to another with the 'Continental circus', subsisting at poverty level but occasionally enjoying a restaurant meal when Lewis happened to get into the prize money. When I returned to England in the early Autumn I had lost twenty pounds in weight after a summer of hard labour and frugal eating.

Assessing the standard of riders towards the back of the field in the smaller capacity classes, I was fairly sure I could compete against some of them without being too disgraced and it was this feeling that I could hold my own which made me want to contest a full season.

So my first full year saw me nicely set up with two Bultacos, new models which Dad received every year from the factory, 125cc and 250cc, and a third Spanish machine bored out to 280cc that we could enter in the 350cc class events. Dad's friendship with Senor Francesco Bulto, then chief of the Bultaco concern, led to this annual arrangement, and our family's Spanish association was completed by the fact that my parents owned a villa at Tarragona, a short journey from Barcelona.

(I seldom visit their beachside retreat, mainly because lying on the sands is not my idea of a holiday. When I have a week off, I prefer to take out my 22-foot speedboat, powered by a 200 hp Mercury outboard, and do a spot of water-skiing off the Sussex coast at Shoreham. That's my idea of a break.)

The £2,000 Stuart Graham wanted for his 125cc Suzuki was a small price to pay, in all honesty, for a machine that would be highly competitive in the world championship. I'd ridden against this twin on a Bultaco single and knew it was a winner in the right hands.

With a loan from my father which I promised to repay as soon as the machine had earned some prize money, the six-year-old ex-works machine was mine and I knew there were others who would have paid double for a machine that possessed a race-winning pedigree. Stuart Graham, retiring from racing, accepted my money first and I knew good times lay ahead. All the money I had in my Post Office savings account went on the Suzuki but Dad and I knew it would represent a good investment.

By current standards going in for Grand Prix racing after two seasons in the saddle would be unheard of. But Europe beckoned and I realised competing with the best in the world could do me nothing but good. I could also combine the trip with a holiday with my parents.

A week before the Spanish 125cc Grand Prix I had won an international in that country and felt full of confidence as I began this end-of-series classic in 1970, even though local hero and world champion Angel Nieto would take some stopping.

Although I had never ridden the twisty Montjuich circuit which wound around the backstreets of Barcelona, I learned quickly enough that I was within half a second of Nieto at the end of practice. As I had previously beaten the tiny Spaniard on his Derbi the week before, I reckoned I could repeat the performance. But as the race settled down into a fairly precise pattern with Nieto and myself leading the field by a huge margin, my Suzuki seemed undergeared for that type of circuit and I had to surrender the victory laurels to Nieto who won by eight seconds. However, second spot in the company of the world's best in that capacity class hammered home the message that I had to reach out regularly for the stiffest kind of available opposition if I wanted to maintain my steady progress.

What also made that meeting stand out in the memory was the 500cc race in which I raced a 360cc Bultaco, which Dad had made up, against the much-revered MV Agusta, piloted by the Italian Angelo Bergamonti. When I qualified just a tenth of a second slower than Bergamonti, who was making his debut on the MV, the crowd were absolutely flabbergasted that some unknown Englishman on a single-cylinder ex-motorcross bike could give a full-blown, factory-backed racer a hard time.

The following year saw me move headlong into a full Grand Prix season on the little Suzuki and it opened my eyes to a different world of racing from one I was used to at home. There were circuits I had never heard of before, let alone seen, and the routine was so different — such as practicing two days before the race instead of on the same morning. The standard of racing was fiercer and the events themselves were longer than I had previously experienced in Britain. World class opposition presented me with a clear examination of my riding skills and by the time that '71 season was over, I knew I could hold my own against the best.

I also contested the 250cc world championship round that year on a Derbi, supplied by the Spanish factory. But the irony was that I was trying to win for them in that class yet doing my best to beat them on the Suzuki in the 125cc rounds. Predictably, it ended with the Derbi dropping out of the 250 series.

In the opening round at the Salzburgring in Austria, I planned to ride three races but was offered a pittance, something like £30 a start, in each of the three events I had entered. That £90 would have had to cover the machine's running costs, fuel, and travelling and living expenses for my mechanic Don Mackay and myself.

On the long journey down to Austria, we had secretly to take some red diesel out of a handy cement mixer in West Germany to put in the Ford Transit when money became tight.

Once at the circuit, I appealed to the organiser to increase my money but he wouldn't budge. He hadn't heard of me, he explained, so how could he justify laying out better money on a completely unknown quantity? He suggested I might get more if I did well in the races but I told him Sunday would be too late for payment. I was absolutely skint and wanted cash to buy food to eat.

I put a proposition to him. 'Pay me £50 for starting in each race if I qualify in the first three each time — but only give me £20 if I'm outside the best three practice times,' I suggested. There was an incentive for both of us. He happily agreed, rubbing his hands at the prospect of having to fork out less than the original agreement. I got my £150 — finishing second fastest in two classes and third in the other.

Since then, this organiser has never forgotten that incident and six years later I had a blazing row with him over the track's medical facilities after a Swiss rider was killed. But we get on all right together now.

That year I took the 34 hp 125cc Suzuki to second place in the world championship, but my racing was run on the proverbial shoestring. Sponsorship was something I knew nothing about. It never occurred to me that you could be given money for putting manufacturers' stickers on the machine's fairing. I was quite content to let companies such as Castrol, Dunlop and Champion advertise on my bikes if they were supplying goods, but I'd never have thought about asking for cash hand-outs for displaying brand names for other people. As a privateer living on the breadline, the glamorous image of Grand Prix racing did not become remotely real for me that year.

After the final practice season, Don would take care of the cycle parts while I would replace the crankshafts. I wouldn't let anyone but myself touch the motor; I felt that only I could take the blame if there was a mechanical disaster. I would complete the task in the early hours of the morning, climb out of the van next day and be ready to race. Sitting on the oil-stained tarmac in my filthy jeans making last-minute pre-race adjustments, I would spot Angel Nieto strolling into the paddock, looking fresh as a daisy after a good night's sleep and happy to know that his team of Derbi factory mechanics had laboured on his behalf to have the bike immaculately prepared ready for his arrival.

Often accompanied by a girl, he would glance in my direction and would appear puzzled that I should be soiling my hands. 'It's all right for you,' I'd shout to him, but there was no malice in my remarks. Angel was making a good living from the sport while I was hoping, one day, to earn enough to live on. But although he was to stop me taking the world title that season, I thoroughly enjoyed the regular dogfights we'd have and I liked being in his company. From him I learned to speak Spanish and now at every Grand Prix we still meet for a chat.

Generally, a good spirit of camaraderie prevails in the paddocks, with riders from every nation happy to offer advice, trade certain secrets and divulge the latest piece of scandal involving a racer and some poor girl who stayed at the track longer than she originally anticipated. (Sweden and Finland were normally the countries where the strong sexual appetites of fit, healthy and predominantly young racers could most easily be satisfied and I have to admit I have taken advantage of the welcoming openness of the ladies in those lands when we have gone there to race Grands Prix. When I made enough money to possess a caravan, the availability of women increased dramatically.)

Another early milestone in the year that launched my career was the first GP win at Francorchamps in Belgium, in which I smashed both race and lap records on my five-year-old Suzuki, at an average speed of over 110 mph. When I followed that up with a double success in Scandinavia, my lead in the championship looked as if it might be enough. Surely Nieto was not going to catch me now even with the superior power output of his Derbi?

What derailed me more than anything in the final run-up to the deciding Spanish GP at Jarama was, firstly, a crash at a non-championship meeting at Hengelo in Holland, where I broke a wrist — my first serious break — and a second accident at Mallory, where I was thrown into the fence after a tyre burst.

The medical team at Leicester Royal Infirmary patched me up and finding nothing wrong, sent me home. How they could have overlooked five broken ribs and compression fracture of three vertebrae defies comprehension but my local doctor immediately recommended a stay in hospital. With the GP five days away, there was no chance! Nothing was going to stop me racing against Nieto in that deciding round and, in great agony, I took the flight to Madrid, paid for out of the fee Kreidler were giving me for the last of the contracted rides on their little 50cc on which I had won a race for them in Czechoslovakia. (That deal was clinched in the toilets at the Belgian GP circuit when I stood side by side with the team manager).

In between the 50cc and 125cc events at the Spanish GP cliff-hanger, one of the fractured ribs began to protrude almost out of my skin as I bent over to sip water from a drinking fountain and it took numerous strips of sticky tape to hold it in position so that I could line up on the grid. But my luck was to be out altogether. Nieto won the race while I lost control of the machine on a patch of oil, spun off but remounted quickly enough to take third place and I was feeling third-rate throughout.

All credit to my Suzuki, though, for it only let me down once in the whole year, a solitary poor piece of welding on a gearbox sprocket.

I emerged from the 1971 session hailed as the rising star of British racing and, with 38 outright race victories behind me and a reputation to expand, my career was taking off in a big way.

Financially, it was a year of constant struggle, with hardship around almost every corner. But I was determined to overcome any handicap. It wasn't easy; I had never thought for one minute that it would be and I wouldn't have wanted it any other way. So I don't want to hear sob-stories from young riders, complaining how tough it is to start racing. I know what it can be like and I am aware of what can be done to pull through. There was no fairy godmother behind me at the begining, only a generous Dad who loaned me enough to buy the Suzuki, money I eventually paid back. I didn't even open a proper bank account until I was 22; any spare cash would be ploughed back into racing, for weekly purchases of vital spares. My commitment to racing was total and I was ambitious to make it to the very top, which I knew would only come through single-minded determination and acceptance of the right opportunities whenever they presented themselves.

In between the moments of glory were sandwiched the black areas, like my only racing visit to the Isle of Man TT where I fell off at Quarter Bridge; the seizure of the semi-works Yamaha at Imola in '72 which left me with a badly-broken left collar-bone that took ages to heal; and then a mishap at Brands the following year where all my toe-nails were torn off my right foot. A front-tyre blow-out had sent me tearing off the Brands track and only by keeping the bike upright with my feet, learnt through trials riding, did I avert a total disaster.

Upon returning to Suzuki hardware, I once again regained my appetite for racing. Poor machinery, team squabbles, disappointing results: little went right during my twelve months with Yamaha in the early seventies and I honestly believed I was no longer finding racing fun. That poor year in '72 taught me a salutary lesson about the dangers of becoming big-headed; over-confidence was the root of my problems.

By this time I believed that basically I had learnt my craft with the small-capacity machines and now wanted to make my name on the high-powered Suzuki triples. These 750cc missiles, the largest and fastest bikes ever constructed, were hitting 180mph and were rated as the most exciting racers to emerge from Japan.

My brother-in-law Paul Smart was contracted to race the Suzuki-3 for the American team and I had highest expectations of riding a similar machine for the British importers. Unfortunately the machine supplied to them arrived via the United States, and it seemed that the 'trick' parts had been replaced by obsolete bits before it crossed the Atlantic.

With a complete rebuild, and a Seeley frame, the 750 was transformed from an old heap into a race-winner, taking me to the coveted European Formula 750 Championship, which I clinched with a carefully-planned second-place ride in the final round at Montjuich Park. This was the evidence I needed to silence the growing band of critics who thought the transition from tiddlers to superbikes to be beyond me. The awards and the successes were coming thick and fast now and I reckon older, established, British riders were beginning to envy the fact that the spotlight had switched from them to me. The pressures, the constant travel, the long hours spent in the workshop might have had their compensations in the shape of a regular Suzuki contract but they heralded the death-knell of my steady relationship with my then girl-friend, Lesley. Apart too long, leading our own separate lives, inevitably there was a split, the termination of a once warm alliance that had begun with a casual chat-up in a London street. But there was never a problem in finding willing replacements!

As a young man with long hair and an obvious disregard for convention, I was seen by the media as being different from the normal identikit picture of the typical motorcycle racer. I tried to be honest and forthright in my replies to journalists' questions and, more often than not, this would lead to banner headlines over stories containing controversial quotes. If it led to greater awareness of my name, so much the better, I thought at the time.

When at the end of '73 I was given the chance to test the prototype Suzuki 500-4 in Japan, the bike had been branded a killer because of its persistent habit of shaking and wobbling when hitting its 175mph top speed along the test-track straights. Far from being terrified by the ordeal in prospect, I tried the new Grand Prix weapon out and returned to the pit grinning broadly. It was a great bike, easily the fastest I had ever ridden. The only thought swimming about my brain was to get that bike crated to Europe to beat Yamaha, who two years previously had turned down my request to ride their 500 in the classics.

I must admit its first year was marked by countless problems. Its handling never improved; gearboxes and drive shafts would break and I was thrown up the road many, many times through mechanical failure. The most horrendous crash took place at Imola once again, where the gearbox jammed. I shot up the track, the Suzuki not far behind, the skin being torn from my shoulders through the gaping holes in my leathers before the bike caught up with me and knocked me unconscious. I awoke to find what appeared to be a covey of nuns in starched white uniforms scrubbing iodine into me, where I had lost large areas of flesh. As well as haemorrhaging an eye, I broke a heel bone, but it was not enough to keep me away from a domestic meeting the next weekend.

What gave me most grounds for concern in the early Suzuki 500-4 days was the accident to a close American friend, Gary Nixon, whom I had recommended to the factory as a potential team-mate for me. They sent for him from the States to test the bike, only for Gary's machine to lock up at 150mph and be instantly rammed by the following machine, with Suzuki test rider Ken Araoka on board. By all accounts, Gary came within a whisker of losing his life and, had he died, I would have given very serious thought to quitting racing. I felt personally responsible because I had set up the opportunity for Gary — a guy with years of experience and as hard as they come — to find out for himself what it was really like and whether or not he could capitalise on the machine's good points, which other riders were not doing at the time. Fellow team-member Paul Smart hated the bike, while third man Jack Findlay seemed unable to ride it quickly enough.

When, after a disappointing year, the Suzuki factory seemed to be losing interest in the project and were on the verge of abandoning further production work, I urged them to continue. 'That will be a good bike. I'll come to Japan to develop it for you and I won't leave until I'm happy with it,' I told the head of the race shop at Hamamatsu.

At the end of five long hard demanding weeks, during which change after change was made, often with no apparent improvement, the machine was reborn and felt every inch a winner.

But the two-wheeled rocket-ship could easily catch you out. I suppose the worst brush with disaster I had pre-Daytona was the incident at Anderstorp in the '74 Swedish GP, when the Suzuki's water pump locked up as the bike was doing 130mph, punched a hole in the bottom of the crankcase and allowed water to escape on to the rear tyre. The machine went sideways and I went into a catch fencing, hotly pursued by the reigning world champion, Giacomo Agostini, who was unable to take avoiding action on his MV Agusta. In spite of slicing the top off a wooden support post with my shoulder in the impact, I escaped most lightly from what could have been a devastating crash.

It was worse for Ago, because his injuries denied him the chance of preventing Phil Read from capturing his world championship title on the other factory MV, which, incidentally, I had had an offer to test in Italy with a view to racing for the factory team in the Grands Prix. Apart from having a mini-test on the superbly engineered machine in a paddock one morning, I never followed up the approach, which came at the time when Suzuki were thinking about abandoning the RG 500 project, the 'baby' I wanted to see develop into a win-

ner. Apart from believing that the Suzuki 500-4 would turn
out to be a world-beater, I felt, as many others did, that the
MV was competing on borrowed time and that developments
in the Far East were taking place far faster than anything
Count Agusta and his men could achieve on a more restricted
budget in Italy. Besides that, I didn't particularly want to get
caught up in the political infighting and petty squabbling that
was known to have gone on between Read and Agostini on
the MV team.

If further evidence was needed that the Suzuki two-stroke
would outstrip the ageing four-stroke MV, then my first victory on it at the non-championship British GP at Silverstone
in 1974 provided it. I took 'Readie' down Hangar Straight and
won comfortably to justify my initial contention that the
Suzuki would be triumphant once the early teething troubles
had been ironed out.

In 1975 came my Daytona disaster, which had some paral-
lels with Silverstone '82 in that in each case the cause was out
of my hands, and my limbs took an awful pasting.

Practising at the banked Florida circuit for the big-money
Daytona race, taking place the following weekend, my 750cc
three-cylinder Suzuki was running perfectly and I was just
looking for a really quick lap time when it all went wrong.
The rear tyre exploded to send me bouncing down the tarmac
at 178mph, like a rag doll. When I looked down at my legs I
could see only one. I thought at first the other had been torn
off. Actually it was broken and behind my line of vision.

If an accident like that can have its compensations, they
lay in the publicity generated. The screening of the Frank
Cvitanovich documentary on British television, which was
made mostly in Daytona and contained the footage of the
crash sequence, together with shock headlines on my injuries
in the national press, made my name more familiar to a wider
audience. Up to that point, I still had not won anything
significant, so all the fuss and publicity I got was slightly
embarrassing.

By now the Daytona crash and the battle to recover from
the multiple injuries are a fading memory. I was simply unfortunate enough to be the victim of a tyre fault while travel-

ling very fast. I think all racers are well aware of the harsher realities they could be faced with from this game. I accepted it as one of the slices of misfortune that always will happen. The bonus, of course, was that it played no small part in boosting public awareness of my name and of the often-dangerous sport in which I was desperately trying to succeed.

With an 18-inch steel rod in my left leg, minus enough skin to upholster a settee, and needing regular pain-killing injections, I had to return to riding a motorcycle at the first opportunity to convince myself I was capable physically of doing the job again. My come-back at Cadwell Park seven weeks after the Daytona smash, told me that all would be well.

Finally, the heartbreak of Daytona was put right behind me within three months when I achieved my first ever Grand Prix victory. What a moment to savour! Right from the start I felt confident I could master the opposition at the Dutch TT at Assen, one of my favourite circuits, and I had the satisfaction of passing Agostini on his 500-4 Yamaha on the side he did not anticipate, to go under the checkered flag first to the deafening roar of the 150,000 crowd.

Every lap, I had sat behind Ago and had made a half-hearted attempt to pass him on the left-hand side each time we entered the corner before the start-and-finish straight. I wanted to fool him into believing I would make my final challenge on that particular line so that he could be ready to counter my late move. He deliberately held a line on the left to block my passage and must have been amazed to see me come through on the right. With his experience he ought to have known that I was setting him up.

When I followed that with a Swedish 500cc GP win at Anderstorp later that season, I fancied I was on the point of take-off. If the world championship was out of Suzuki's reach that year, then surely 1976 would bring the culmination of three years' development work on the 500-4 RG programme. However, I hadn't anticipated cracking my right knee when I banged it against a Mallory Park kerb in winning the Race of the Year, and then severing the knee joint a week later when performing a wheelie demonstration on a Bultaco for a fan at Cadwell Park.

I declined immediate surgery in the local hospital in London. I preferred the best medical attention money could buy. My career was at stake and I wasn't sure that the necessary five-hour operation could have been performed anywhere but at a top London clinic. As I entered the operating theatre the surgeon had advised me there was only a fifty-fifty chance of restoring the knee joint to its original condition. But after brilliant surgery, which involved inserting two screws into the back of the knee, I knew I would be back to normal after a winter's rest — ready to tackle the world championship once more.

5
CHAMPAGNE
YEARS

My preparation for the '76 season, the season in which I was to win the world championship at 500cc level, centred on fighting to recapture my fitness after my leg operation.

Even though I depended heavily on two hawthorn walking sticks to get from one lady to another, my favourite part of the rehabilitation programme was to try to bed as many women as possible. Being sidelined for almost six months gave me the opportunity to do what I enjoyed most of all at that time — chase crumpet. I cast all thoughts of bikes from my mind during the winter of '75 as I set about the constant and demanding daily struggle to be with girls who took my fancy. Those were the bachelor days, when I lived life to the full with every day presenting the chance to do something more outrageous than the one before.

This was to be my final fling, the last period of playing around, and if I were to list some of the exploits that I got up to, I would make myself blush. Since settling down to a steady relationship with Steph, I have never once yearned for those wild times: the days of the paddock groupies; the passionate notes waiting for me when I returned to hotels after a race; the women who simply wanted to experience sex with a celebrity. All that is behind me now.

Back in the early seventies, I had made a deliberate attempt to become known beyond the normal audience of spectators who followed racing. While other sports produced household names, motorcycle-racing's heroes never received the exposure their feats deserved, and consequently there was nothing to awaken potential major sponsors to the fact that here was a good sport with the appeal to capture the imagination of all kinds of people, especially the free-spending young.

Let's face it: most riders and most races appeal only to the motorcycling fraternity. That doesn't amount to many millions. The possibilities of attracting a decent advertising contract were virtually nil while my name was known only to the motorcycling fraternity. Take Faberge for example. I would never have figured in their plans simply as a motorcyclist. As it is, I have even done an Italian television campaign for them: they clearly realised that I had established an image that appealed to many Italian households.

I reckon I finally destroyed the popular concept of a biker when I was pictured in the Sun, modelling underwear and accompanied by a half-naked lady. This wasn't quite what traditional bike enthusiasts had come to expect, but I'm sure it helped to undermine the myth that all those who rode motorcycles are dumb, dirty and definitely undesirable.

Now my reputation as a man about town, hitting the night spots, dining in good restaurants and being seen with pretty girls all added to the image. The social activities, I might add, were not planned to attract attention; I would have behaved just the same and been up to just as many naughty deeds had I been Barry Sheene, van driver, instead of a young bike-racer brimming over with ambition. The right places to be seen in by the national press happened to be the places I liked going to anyway. Places like Tramp tend to attract a high proportion of professionals with something of a reputation for waving two fingers at the establishment.

To be truthful, I had always enjoyed my social life to the full. Now, though, it was coming under close media scrutiny and to hear of a top racer smoking, drinking and stopping out all night with women upset the die-hards.

There may be unwritten rules, to some people, on what a sportsman can or can't do. What difference does it make if, at the end of the day, he neither upsets anyone nor loses his form? There was no doubt that my activities — and they were as varied as they were intense — never interfered with my performance on the track. But they did help to tune in sponsors outside motorcycling to the fact that it was time to re-examine the idea that a bike is just a poor man's racing car.

It helps to have friends around when accidents necessitate

long periods of convalescence and, towards the end of 1975, Piers Forrester kindly allowed me to share his Chelsea town house while I was recovering from my busted knee. Piers, an Old Harrovian, was a remarkable character. The grandson of the fifth Marquis of Ormonde, he had driven racing-cars, taken part in long-distance motorcycle endurance tests and enjoyed free-fall parachuting. I suppose his biggest claim to fame was his association with Princess Anne before she married. We shared a devil-may-care outlook on life and we got on as fabulously as a pair of brothers.

Piers, because he always moved in the highest social circles, would receive frequent invitations to cocktail parties hosted by 'Hooray Henries', the sort who lived and dressed well on their fathers' money. I'd be taken along. The well-spoken ladies who always shopped in the top stores and were destined to marry into money were known as the 'Mayfair Marines' or 'Hyde Park Commandos' and I guess these hostesses regretted including us on their guest lists. We tended to misbehave. Before moving on to a restaurant for dinner and then to a club like Tramp for dancing, we would go along just to have a good laugh and to bring the more snobbish down to earth. Later, Piers lost control of his machine at Brands and was killed. I openly wept on hearing of his crash. We were that close.

Then, at the end of that year, as my broken leg rapidly mended, the press picked up the tale about me and Stephanie Maclean, a highly attractive model with cover-girl looks who just happened to be married.

It was the Frank Cvitanovich documentary of my Daytona crash that first brought me to her attention. The red, white and blue Team Suzuki leathers I was wearing looked attractive enough for her to want to model them. I had first noticed her in the Old Spice television commercials, but was completely mesmerised by her when she cruised into Tramp with her husband. I was just leaving the club when she came in and I couldn't get her out of my mind for the rest of the night. I knew her agent Lorraine Ashton, who gave Steph my number and she phoned me a few days later to enquire about trying on the Suzuki leathers. She looked superb in them—and her husband, a professional photographer, recorded the moment on film. The romance developed from the October, 1975, photo session and the bond between us has continued to strengthen.

I had never before been involved with a married woman. It was more or less forbidden, in my book. The prospect of being nabbed by an irate husband didn't particularly appeal and, besides, there were ample supplies of warm-hearted single women. But when I met Steph, my self-made rules about married women were ignored, and our relationship quickly blossomed. She was perfect for me. And since I knew about her husband and her child, there was no big shock waiting to hit me.

With a massive list of conquests behind me, I knew I had completed all the running around I had ever wanted. I had tried everything I had read about and a whole lot more besides. Two women sharing my bed was old hat as far as I was concerned. But, at last, here was my dream lady. She fitted perfectly my picture of what the ideal woman should be.

I didn't break up Steph's marriage. Although she and her husband Clive were still living together, the relationship between them had already terminated. So there was no hassle when the news leaked out that I had been escorting Steph. Of course, I was named as the 'other man' when divorce proceedings were heard in court, but that wasn't unexpected nor did it involve any bitter wrangling between the various parties. We all three seemed happy at the outcome. It was a relief when the secret came out into the open after what had been a difficult time for the pair of us as we tried to keep our friendship discreet.

It helped being mobile again. Now that my 18-month driving ban was over, I eagerly made the most of the Rolls Royce Silver Shadow I had bought that year when the earnings started to roll in. The disqualification from driving was the result of a foolish act on my part. When I lived near Wisbech, a friend and I visited a night club in neighbouring King's Lynn and I admit we had enjoyed a few rounds of drinks. Volunteering to drive home, I was horrified to be in a collision with an oncoming car that was pulling out to overtake a parked vehicle. Although there was very little damage to the cars or their occupants, I did have some fragments of glass in my eye which I wanted to sluice out at home as quickly as I could before reporting the accident to the police. Before I could get inside my house, a squad car pulled me up and I was breathalysed.

The sequel at Lynn Crown Court resulted in my licence being suspended for the standard twelve months plus a further six months on the totting up of endorsements procedure. I also had to take my driving test again at the end of the ban. This rotten news was only made bearable by the many offers from associates willing to chauffeur me around the country.

Since then I flatly refuse to consume any form of alcohol if I have to drive anywhere. Nobody who hasn't lost his licence can understand what it's like. All the advertising campaigns in the world don't work. They certainly didn't affect me. I'm glad now that I lost my licence, because it damn well taught me a lesson. Drinking and driving is a mug's game.

It is a hard enough job keeping clear of the law in other ways. The speeding, for example, which has earned me numerous endorsements. You might think I'd be let off with a ear-bashing by the police when they recognise who they have pulled up. But unfortunately it doesn't happen like that. I just get nicked.

I was travelling in a stream of traffic to Shoreham one day on a dual carriageway with at least 50 cars ahead of and behind me. Even though I was moving at the same pace as the traffic, which, according to the police, was 45 mph in a 30 mph restriction zone, I was the one singled out by the cops operating the radar speed trap. 'Why me when we were all moving at the same speed?' I asked. 'I just picked you, that's why,' said the patrolman.

I was once stopped near Gatwick Airport on the motorway early one morning, doing 100 mph. The road was empty and I admit I was motoring quite hard. I can even remember seeing the police patrol car pull off its roadside ramp to tail me before I was flagged down and booked. What I should have done, perhaps, was to lock on the brakes to send the Granada sideways. 'Didn't you see the cat crossing the road, officer?' I would have said. As it was, there was another black mark on my licence. I came near to a second driving ban after another occasion, but my solicitor managed to dispute the speed restriction in force at the time.

Even so, it has not altered the way I drive. I happen to think that 70 mph is a foolish limit. Every car is made to do at least that and when you return to this country after driving abroad the restriction here seems so frustrating. I came back from the Austrian Grand Prix, 700 miles in seven and a half hours, only to get pinched on the motorway not ten miles from my home.

With Stephanie by my side, and the big front page splash about to break over our love affair, I entered the '76 season supremely confident that the Suzuki could take me to the title provided it held together from a reliability point of view.

Pushing the bike to start was a problem because of the limitations of the left leg with the steel rod inside it, and it often meant my starts were far from impressive. But in the end, it all worked out magnificently.

Though a misfire kept me in second place in the Belgian round, it was won by my team mate of that year, John Williams. He crashed heavily in practice for the following round in Sweden. Travelling not far behind, I immediately stopped to help. Dirt appeared to be blocking his air passage and I scooped out what I could before the ambulance arrived. He survived that afternoon only to lose his life later on the road circuit at Dundrod, in Northern Ireland.

By the time we reached the Dutch TT, I had already won three consecutive GPs. Anderstorp was the title-clincher. After that, Agostino, then reigning champion, virtually resigned. Anderstorp and the title justified my asking Suzuki GB to raise their retainer for the following year. I received an increase — and, at 25, welcomed the opportunity to wallow in the fame and glory world champions enjoy.

In 1977, the pressure on me to retain the title was intensified, I felt, when Yamaha contracted my friend Johnny Cecotto, a Venezuelan with loads of talent who had won the 350cc world championship in his first season, and American

Steve Baker, quiet, thoughtful but highly-rated throughout Europe. The opposition, on paper, looked far tougher this time, and judging by performances in the opening round at sun-baked San Carlos in Venezuela, Yamaha had worked on their 500-4 all winter to give it more power.

When I tested my Suzuki in Japan during the close season, the technicians had implemented one or two changes to help boost performance but nothing had been dramatically improved. Better aerodynamically-designed streamlining was a step in the right direction but it was generally felt the disc-valve Suzuki, with minor alterations to the suspension, had shown itself to be good enough the previous year not to need major surgery. The boys involved in development work at the Suzuki racing shop in Japan, with whom my association went back four years, would listen to suggestions put to them, but there was a feeling that they were wary about making too many modifications to the carburation because, in this area, they knew that my extensive knowledge and experience might have led me to pinpoint construction flaws.

Before the start of the season I took Steph to Japan with me and, being a tall blonde amidst a nation of tiny, dark-haired women, she would draw glances everywhere we travelled. The companionship was welcome because I dislike going to Japan on my own. Not only had I never before had a girl friend I rated worth taking to the other side of the world, but I genuinely wanted to be in Steph's company after spending long hours sorting out the new bikes. Besides, a visitor to Japan stands little chance of meeting an accommodating lady unless lots of yen change hands.

The season started well, with victory in the opening Venezuelan round, as I came through from last away from the grid to overhaul Baker as he tired in the intense heat. Then the steel pin in my leg, legacy of the Daytona accident, was removed under the gaze of television cameras with a hammer and instruments that closely resembled a pair of mole grips, and my body began to feel in much better shape.

The following round of the 500cc Grand Prix series at the Salzburgring in Austria saw an undercurrent of unease and disquiet over the whole world championship structure come

to a head. At that meeting, I said that FIM stood for the
Federation of Inconsiderate and Indifferent Morons, because
of the callous approach taken by all those involved in running the event. Flag marshals, perhaps the most important
officials at a race event, appeared to lack basic instruction,
and arrangements over medical facilities left a great deal to be
desired. A huge crowd congesting approach roads meant that
the journey time of an ambulance carrying an injured rider to
the nearest hospital for urgent treatment could be critically
prolonged. The medical team at the track appeared to lack
the necessary experience to deal with emergency cases, while
the circuit's helicopter — a Jet Ranger — standing by in the
paddock was clearly too small to accommodate a stretcher.

A few of us, acting on behalf of the other factory runners,
were accused of being unreasonable in our demands for
better all-round medical facilities. The FIM claimed the
situation was acceptable, and it took the death of a rider in a
multiple pile-up to drive home the inadequacies of the circuit.

We refused to contest the 500cc race because it was apparent no action was going to be taken and I was most
disappointed with the FIM's attitude. Double the amount of
start money was offered but only a handful of uncaring riders
decided to line up for the event.

Angel Nieto, looking after the interests of the smaller-
capacity riders, and myself were cited as ring-leaders of this
'disturbance' to the FIM's pool of mediocrity and we were
'severely reprimanded' and fined. I never bothered to pay the
fine and completely ignored the possibility that the FIM
might take away my racing licence, which was within their
power. Had they attempted to do so, I would have gone to
the Human Rights Court in Strasbourg basing my case on the
fact that my living was being denied me because I had asked
for first aid arrangements that could decide whether a man
lived or died.

This dispute roused a number of riders to form the Association of Professional Riders whose aim, with the help of promotional experts IMG, led by Mark McCormack, was to try
to achieve a better deal for international racers competing in
the world championships. I understand I was about the only

rider not to sign up to join the revolution, which I refused to do basically because I thought it was a total waste of time. It is impossible to have a successful organisation when its members are incapable of displaying a united front on the major issues and I was convinced they wouldn't stick together when complex issues had to be faced. I explained that I would do whatever I thought seemed right, and if a particular circuit seemed to me dangerous, I wouldn't ride there unless specially ordered to do so by the team paying me.

All I was intent on achieving was a second title for Suzuki. I won the West German, Italian and French rounds in succession. The biggest threat, Cecotto, was unluckily sidelined at the Austrian GP with injuries, so the signs were encouraging. The Italian success was the first time I had finished first at Imola in seven outings there. The number seven has always been a figure I consider lucky, and even though racing numbers designated by the FIM should correspond to the placings in the class standings in the previous year's championship, I have had 7 on my machines since 1974. In this game, you have to take every piece of luck that's going. I am superstitious enough to look for lucky omens, which may seem silly but is now a matter of habit. Even the hotel rooms and pit-lane garages I book should have a number that is a multiple of seven or that adds up to seven.

To the incredible delight of the partisan crowd, local hero Wil Hartog beat me in the Dutch round at Assen but I was pleased with my showing, because after the warming-up lap it was discovered that the wheels of my RG500 Suzuki were seven millimetres out of line, which accounted for its poor handling. There was nothing to be done in the few seconds left before the race and I set off in the rain with the pack, livid at the mistake in my pre-race preparation. I had asked the mechanics to put on a special-cut intermediate tyre which would have worked wonders had it not been raining. As it was, until the track dried out near the end I was unable to make much headway and it was only on the final lap that I really began to cut back Hartog's lead.

In the next race counting for world championship points, a hornet attempted to halt my progress. I was trying to log a good practice time on the then long and super-fast Francor-champs circuit, in the heart of the Ardennes. As I spotted the creature heading for me while I was accelerating away from the pits I quickly moved my head aside because I didn't want a splattered mess that might impair my vision on the perspex face mask. The hornet flew down the neck of my leathers, and even though I braked as fast as I dared, I couldn't capture the beast before it stung me. A doctor later removed the sting with tweezers and gave me an injection to neutralise the effect. Unfortunately, the antibiotics caused my right hand to swell up on raceday, which made throttle control a precarious operation, but the handicap failed to prevent me from winning my fifth GP of the season, eleven seconds ahead of Baker, who was coming under a lot of pressure from Yamaha to try to break the Suzuki domination.

I achieved another maximum fifteen points in Sweden — always a successful hunting ground for me, partly because by the stage of the season when this round takes place, the gremlins with the bike have been eradicated — which left me in the happy position of needing only a sixth place in the Finnish GP — a track which crosses a railway line — to take the title again.

The Imatra race in Finland gave us the first mechanical problems of the year. In practice, the head gasket kept blowing, and the bike would lose the coolant out of its system. In the actual race, the bike overheated dramatically, the temperature-gauge needle winding right off the clock. When we checked at the end — after I had finished sixth — there wasn't a drop of water in the radiator.

What was impressive was the improved performance of the privately-entered RG500s now available. On a good day there seemed little difference between the standard model and my factory mount. The title that year could easily have been won by a privately-entered Suzuki. It made life that much tougher, and I knew it would get no better the following year.

Winning a second successive world title here added to my store of memories from Finland. I have had lots of good times there in the past, on the track and all.

There was the time my big rival Johnny Cecotto, now racing cars, and I were splashing about with two girls in a bath in an Imatra hotel after the completion of qualifying. The hotel manager, obviously summoned by irate guests to investigate the commotion, opened the door with his pass key and we sprayed him down with water from a hosepipe. Fortunately the guy's strong sense of humour held out, and we got away with it.

It was Finland also where I became involved in the episode of the exploding toilets. The shed in the paddock which housed the lavatories for all the riders, mechanics and their families was a disgusting place. The wives and kids who were forced to brave the smell and the germs suffered most. It was totally unfair for anyone to have to use these facilities — and the organisers of the race meeting seemed most reluctant to do anything about them.

So a few riders and myself hatched a plot that would leave the promoters no choice but to build a whole block of new toilets. After we had poured ten gallons of 100-octane fuel down the loos, my fellow conspirators lost their bottle at the last minute, and so it was left to me to strike the match. The bogs went up with a deafening bang and the whole lot went skyways, finishing up in the adjoining lake. We had previously put a car and caravan across the entrance gates to the paddock to stop the fire engine from getting through to put out the flames. It wasn't necessary — there was nothing left to save.

On another funny occasion, this time at Brno in Czechoslovakia, I was with Tepi Lansivuori, a Finnish racer with a droll sense of humour. Czechoslovakia, like East Germany, is a country I detest because of its Communist regime. You only have to say a word out of place against the state and you're punished for it. What Tepi and I did was meant to be a kick against Communism. It wasn't anything spectacular, just a matter of driving along the main street with a road traffic cone on the top of our car. It was our way of showing that someone dared to stand up against the authorities. We were stopped and questioned by the police but in the end were waved on. A Czech citizen would risk being locked away in a

mental hospital for doing something like that. The
Communist way of life with its suppression of personal
freedom is something few people in Britain can fully appreciate. If someone was to sample their system and come home
to say how much he enjoyed it, I would personally sponsor
him to live over there.

Fortunately there is no longer a 500cc world championship
race in Czechoslovakia, which means I don't have to compete
behind the Iron Curtain again. I well remember racing at the
Brno round-the-house circuit. When I complained about the
vast number of dangerous sections, my hints about a possible
boycott were met with cries of 'think of all the people you'll
let down'. If they were really looking after the interests of the
Czechs they could have built a proper, safe, circuit with the
money collected from a 200,000 attendance.

Perhaps the craziest stunt I was involved in took place in
Italy when we were preparing for a big 200cc race at Imola.
Kenny Roberts and Gene Romero, the American racers, were
in a hire car with me which Kenny was driving somewhat
erratically due, in no small way, to the fact that Gene was
operating the pedals while I was wrenching the handbrake to
spin the back around. The rent-a-racer Fiat careered down a
grassy bank and turned upside down in a muddy canal. Gene
scrambled out as best he could but my foot was caught under
the handbrake. I panicked a little, but eventually pulled free.
Kenny was trapped and cried out for assistance. We eased
him out as the water rapidly rose inside the car. It was a close
call. Looking back on the incident after we returned to our
hotel, we realised the stupidity of the prank. Someone could
have lost his life and it could easily have been me.

At Silverstone, in '77, for the first mainland British Grand
Prix counting towards the world championship, I arrived as
champion, but my factory Suzuki was plagued with head
gasket trouble. It would blow every time I went out to seek a
qualifying time. So in desperation, as the seconds to the final
qualifying session ticked away, I grabbed Steve Parrish's
standard production Suzuki, without a screen. Steve was in
the Heron Suzuki-GB team as the third rider.

'Is that thing OK?' I shouted to the chief mechanic, Martyn

Ogborne.

'Sure, but remember it's just a standard machine,' he replied.

At last I was able to do two successive laps and the machine was good enough to give me a pole position, about a half second in front of Cecotto on his Yamaha. However, I went out of the race, predictably, with a recurrence of the persistent head gasket trouble on my pukka works bike. Suzuki had refused to provide me with a standard machine, which I believed was a better proposition than my mount at that stage. It was significant that Steve 'Stavros' Parrish put in the fastest lap in the race on his standard bike and looked set to win until he fell at Copse. When I came in angrily, dripping with scalding water after the head gasket blew, I shot up pit lane and deliberately ran the bike into the garage wall to bend the forks and chassis. They'd have to supply an ordinary bike next time!

Now I was world champion again, people tried to put one over me. Other riders seemed to try just that little bit harder to earn the satisfaction of finishing in front. Some of the spectators were beginning to resent my continuing run of success and it was never a surprise to find the occasional letter from a race fan in *Motor Cycle News* and *Motor Cycle Weekly* complaining about a selection of defects in my character, from asking too much money to not wanting to devote time to the followers, something which was emphatic-ally untrue. I lost no sleep. And when sections of certain crowds voiced their disapproval of me, I wouldn't react violently.

But at Oliver's Mount, a compact, twisty enthusiasts' circuit perched high on a hill overlooking the popular seaside resort of Scarborough, the behaviour of some of the capacity crowd got out of hand. This was in the period when Mick Grant, a Yorkshireman through and through, carried the torch for all northerners. Since the meeting was held on his territory, I anticipated some healthy rivalry. But the inter-national meeting in '77 seemed to attract the soccer-style hooligan element, who let their emotions carry them away. They poked sticks through fencing as I rode past, and the odd beer-can would be aimed in my direction as I led their hero on his 750 Kawasaki triple.

Another thing that annoyed me about the bad scenes at Scarborough that year and spoilt the enjoyment the meeting usually offers me was the bad language. Now I'm no angel and my conversation is invariably peppered with expletives but I always try to mind my manners when talking in front of kids. I could actually hear the more abusive and vociferous groups swearing at me as I went through the slower sections and I hated to think what impression it left on the children and families who were there.

People like this would seem more at home at a football match. Not only were their antics offensive, dangerous and clearly designed to slow me down or to frighten me, but they attracted the type of publicity racing could well do without.

I have often been asked why I race at Scarborough, a course which in some ways has similarities to the closed-road circuits in Europe about which I have been so critical in the past.

I don't think the Oliver's Mount circuit is dangerous, provided you ride there with the necessary safety margins in mind. That's not to say I'll travel slowly there, even though in the downhill sections to the final hairpin I'll almost dawdle. I've broken all the race and lap records during my many visits. But it is a short circuit, with good access all round, and its medical facilities and scope for speedy ambulance service to the local hospital, makes it comparable, from the safety aspect, with other tracks. It may be narrow with some steep gradients but all corners are well protected with an abundance of straw bales. As with any other circuit, if there are sections which you can't tackle with confidence, it's up to you to ride through those sections at the pace best suited to you. You can make up the lost time in other stretches, where there is less likelihood of hurting yourself.

As well as waging war against an increased number of highly-competitive bikes, I was also having to contend with Vernon Cooper, chairman of UK road racing's organising body and the front man of motorcycle sport policies in this country.

We had crossed swords in the aftermath of the Austrian GP chaos, and later that year, my blood boiled when he was quoted as saying, 'Enormous amounts of money paid to some riders results in little or no funds being available to riders who justifiably need to make a living from their professional riding ability. After the big names have had their cut, there is often little left to share among the lesser-knowns.'

To him, professional riders were those who race at weekends and do a job during the other five days, not those whose sole income comes from this sport. It was acceptable for him to be a wealthy man and live a life of luxury, but in his eyes, racers should be subservient, peasants to whom he can successfully dictate and on whom he can foist his opinions.

How can a person who has never actually raced set himself up as the sole judge of the safety of racing circuits? Can he ride a motor bike? Perhaps it's irrelevant, but I do feel that he objects to riders like myself who have made something out of the sport, forgetting what we have put into it in terms of increased public awareness and greater entertainment. My jousts with Cooper were to be prominently featured in the weekly specialist press, who pursued our verbal battles with unstinting enthusiasm. I am sorry if any of my remarks wounded his pride but I enjoyed every opportunity to reply to his comments that were invariably directed at me.

When Kenny Roberts decided to give the world championship a try in 1978, I was anything but worried about his coming. I was said to be quaking in my boots and tossing in my sleep at night in expectation of someone who might mess up my victory programme. I hate to disappoint all the rumourmongers, but it has to be said that I just regarded him as one more rider to compete against; one more to beat.

What annoyed me at that time were his comments about Steve Baker, suggesting ways in which he should have ridden the '77 season for Yamaha so that the company might be successful. Those remarks condemning Steve's ability were responsible, I think, for Steve's losing his factory support.

If I made any derogatory comments about Kenny, it was his criticism of Steve Baker that prompted me to do so. But I knew I could get Kenny agitated by continually telling the press that Johnny Cecotto was the guy certain to provide me with the sternest challenge where my 500cc title was concerned. That approach was calculated to get Kenny going, and it worked every time.

I realised that Kenny had every chance of winning the title, but considered that I was an equally strong contender. The prospect of his arrival didn't worry me unduly. Even though I had won 23 of the 35 races I had entered that year — crashing once, at Snetterton, when the brake pads fell out — the pundits were forecasting that 1978 would be the end of my reign at the top. King Kenny was coming with his factory Yamaha, and if I believed everything the press said about the greatness of the man, I should have been on the brink of suicide.

I had raced against him before at home and abroad and the prospect of facing him as I went for a third consecutive world title would not have been daunting had we both been on machines with identical performance levels. There was so much bullshit floating around about how superior Roberts was as a rider, that I threw down a public challenge for the pair of us to have a head-to-head race on standard, out-of-the-crate machines, with a £5,000 prize at stake. Let him put his money where his mouth is, I thought. Needless to say, he didn't accept the offer — and five years later I was still waiting. All I've ever asked is to be on equal machinery with the other top riders — and I was still asking that same question when I piled up at Silverstone.

Even away from the track, headlines were being made wherever I went. Some were less then welcome! Invited to be a judge at the Miss World contest in '77, I naturally accepted with alacrity. The ceremony went well, with Mary Stavins — later to become the girl friend of footballing hero George Best — being voted the most beautiful woman. But at the banquet afterwards, which I went to in spite of being jet-lagged after my return from Japan that day, a photographer asked me to pose with the winner just as the main course arrived, which would have gone a long way towards curing the hunger pangs that followed a day without food. The persistent photographer went away when he discovered that I had no intention of deserting my meal in favour of a publicity photograph, but he sent over a colleague who repeatedly requested a picture of me dancing with Mary Stavins.

'You don't want me to dance with her do you?' I said to Stephanie, who was seated next to me, seeking back-up from her so that the photographer would get the message that all I wanted to do at that moment was to eat. Steph, somewhat fed up by the attention of the pressmen, went out to the car while I, determined to eat what was before me, cleared the remaining Brussels sprouts from my plate.

I should have chosen my words more carefully, because the daily papers ran stories the next day about Steph blowing a fuse over me being asked to dance with Miss World in preference to her. There was absolutely no row or lover's tiff between us and my remarks had been totally misconstrued by the press. If I had wanted to dance with Miss World, or even her mother, no-one would have stopped me. But of course I would have left myself open to suggestions that I might be giving her more than just the pleasure of a few laps of the ballroom. There's always some controversy surrounding the Miss World competition, usually in the name of publicity. That year, unfortunately, it happened to involve me.

6
GOODBYE
SUZUKI

The Suzukis I had tested in Japan, developed to keep Kenny Roberts and the Yamaha at bay in '78, indicated that the power characteristics had been improved. A stepped cylinder arrangement, which lowered the bike's centre of gravity, produced a better power curve. Sadly, though, the modifications were later to prove insufficient to match the speed of the Yamaha.

The season began well enough with a relatively comfortable win for me in the blistering 109° heat of San Carlos, in the opening Venezuelan Grand Prix.

By the time I left Caracas, the Venezuelan capital I love so much, I was in trouble. I had begin to shiver at the airport, and I felt unwell on the seven-hour flight home. As the virus — later diagnosed as Bornholm's Disease — developed, the variation in body temperature was enormous. One minute I was cold as an iceberg, the next I was sweating. Overtaken as I was by total lethargy, not long after getting up in the morning I would doze off on the couch.

In a race, I would start to perspire after three laps that had seemed like 130 laps and would gradually lose the ability to concentrate. As soon as I went to bed, at 11, I would drop off to sleep instantly, only to wake up two hours later to vomit in the bathroom for no apparent reason.

The tiredness and lack of energy were major problems, since they were major handicaps to my chances of lasting any kind of race through to the checkered flag. Desperate to free myself from the bug, I sought advice from almost every known medical source, from my own Harley Street specialist to a unit dealing in tropical diseases. I was also suffering from a blinding pain across my chest, though X-rays failed to reveal anything amiss. Medical opinion suggested it was a virus which might stay with me for an indefinite period. I was prescribed a whole package of vitamin tablets and was reassured that the illness would desert me in its own good time. But it really knocked the stuffing out of me and I became so depressed I wondered if I ever would return to my normal state.

When I was offered a week on the luxury yacht belonging to Heron Corporation chief Gerald Ronson, I gratefully jumped at the chance. Gerald and his wife Gail, Stephanie and I, set off to cruise the Mediterranean and I figured the complete rest would cure me of the virus.

On the second day, out on the sea, miles from anywhere, I woke up feeling so much better. It was as if someone had removed a shadow from me. I felt much sharper, more enthusiastic about life and was serenely content to spend the following days swimming, snorkelling, eating and sleeping in the vigorous manner in which I had previously led life to the full.

That holiday in the sun allowed me to return to racing with a huge grin on my face. 'I'll show you now,' was my attitude as I straddled a bike feeling spot-on for the first time in months.

The bug, however, ruined my '78 race-plan strategy, although four third places and — restored again to tip-top health — yet another win in Sweden put me within three points of the overall lead in the series. So much could have hinged on a good result in the Finnish GP, the penultimate round. I was quickest in practice to start with, so anything was possible. But I pulled in perturbed. There was so much vibration being transmitted from the motor, there seemed every likelihood that a crank was about to go west.

The relationship with the Suzuki parent was turning sourer by the minute in that Imatra paddock. After completing the last of the four timed practice sessions I changed out of my sticky leathers and ambled over to the team tent to inform the Japanese mechanics — flown over to maintain the championship bid — that one of the crankshaft bearings in my RG500 hinted it was on the brink of breaking up.

Immediately, quizzical frowns appeared on the Japanese faces as if they doubted my claim. After all, they had designed these particular components, back in the Land of the Rising Sun, and so they should know best.

'How you achieve fastest qualifying time if bearings not good?' they queried in broken English, unwilling to strip down the engine to check out my fears. I insisted my diagnosis was correct and told them in no uncertain terms what my feelings would be, when there was a mechanical failure in the next day's race because of the bearings. There was no doubt in my mind.

When the race began, I cut through the field and, on the fifth lap, just as I took the lead in full control of the situation, the bike packed up...through crankshaft bearing failure.

The blame for my failure, and the loss of my strong position for title contention, had to be laid at the door of the Japanese employees, but words were unnecessary when I flicked back the canvas awning flap upon returning to the camp. The silent, unresponsive bike said it all for me. The memory of their costly intransigence stuck with me from then on.

So '78 proved to be a rub-out year on account of the Yamaha's extra pace, my early season illness and the fact that there were insufficient events left, once I recovered, to do anything about challenging Yamaha's new dominance.

Then, of course, Suzuki, in blind panic, felt that drafting new riders to bolster their world championship challenge might do the trick. What it meant, however, was that they were dividing their attention amongst a greater number of riders. Their approach to overcoming the severe Yamaha challenge was far from impressive and their misplaced confidence in roping in the lanky Dutchman Wil Hartog, and Virginio Ferrari, a firebrand from Italy, did not bring the desired results they regarded as easily attainable. All it did was alienate me further from Suzuki as the team spirit between the factory and me continued to deteriorate.

Had I gone to the Nurburgring that season with a few more points in the bag from the round at Silverstone, it might have

been more of a cliffhanger, especially in view of Kenny
Roberts' cautious approach to the West German circuit.

There was still an outside chance that I could snatch the
title at the final attempt, but there was no way I was going to
ride hard round the Nurburgring. The obstacles, man-made
and natural, were bad enough; but the sheer length of the
circuit, which increased the chances of falling where no
ambulances were stationed, made it, for me, a nightmare.

My only hope was for Roberts to retire from the race; and
for me to finish as high as fourth. That was the best effort I
intended to make; there was certainly no possibility of me
going all out to beat Roberts round here. I gather Kenny
wasn't prepared to risk much either, and wanted to do just
enough to get in the points. But he took third, scooped the
title, and went on to have a huge celebration party.

I shook hands with him at the end of the race and offered
my own personal congratulations. He had ridden well
through the year and had won the championship fair and
square, even though his Yamaha could blitz anything coming
out of the corners to give him an advantage that made
everyone envious.

It wasn't a case of making excuses. I genuinely was sick and
I had told the Suzuki camp they could not expect me to do
better than finish around third or fourth each time, which is
what I was achieving. That was the best I could do at the
moment, I explained, knowing everything would eventually
get better. Suzuki, so anxious not to hand over the precious
title to their big rivals, looked for any kind of solution and
consulted Hartog and Ferrari who, after the season closed,
appeared to hold some sway with the factory technicians.

Hartog was never one of my favourite riders and I fancy
many others in the Grand Prix 'circus' shared my low opinion
of him. Instead of really saying what he thought, he would
tell people what he thought they wanted to hear. When he
announced his retirement in 1981, the whole paddock almost
jumped for joy. He was then the riders' representative.
Everything, according to him, was perfect with the way the
sport was being organised. Unsafe circuits, poor money,
unsatisfactory conditions? There were no complaints in Wil's

eyes. He was just the sort of man to appeal to the FIM.

When I was speaking on behalf of the racers, the CCR — the road racing committee of the FIM — hated the sight of me. I would always pipe up at meetings to put forward the riders' viewpoint or else to disagree with a recommendation that the riders felt threatened them. These constant interruptions to the flow of items on the agenda quite clearly annoyed the established members of the committee who often wanted to dismiss, without debate, certain of my queries.

'We must get on,' would be their terse comment to my query on a burning topic. But this involves people's lives, I would say.

Hartog was a 'yes' man, bowing and scraping to the authorities. When he was out testing the Suzuki in Japan, I complained first about the machine's head angles, then about one thing after another which seemed unsatisfactory. But Hartog seemed keen not to offend the Japanese in any way.

'This is a wonderful bike — the best I've ever ridden,' he would comment. They were hearing what they had hoped to hear, but the Japanese never take anything for granted and they later learnt that my impressions of the modified bike were far more accurate than his.

Frankness has landed me in hot water more than once. Rather than licking backsides, I've always said what I felt, and consequently my remarks have upset people. Throughout my racing career , I know the feelings I have expressed have not always gone down well with lots of folks. But I've been brought up always to be honest; the truth will come out in the end, so why tell someone something is wonderful when eventually they are going to be disappointed to hear it is not so great after all?

It was when Hartog began to criticise the machine later in the year that the Japanese began to raise an eyebrow or two. By gushing about the Suzuki to begin with, he must have imagined they would look after him for evermore. He should have told the truth about the bike's weaknesses right from the start and made the Suzuki technicians rate him in the category assigned to me when I complained — an arsehole. When Suzuki elbowed him out, it proved it wasn't worth giving the

Japanese all that bullshit.

It was clear that Suzuki were paranoid about losing the '78 championship to Yamaha. But the bike was OK in '78 and I felt there was little modification needed. What perhaps cost them the chance of having a hat-trick of world championship wins was my illness, which meant I was unable to screw out the best from the bike. Once I was back to good health, I began winning again.

When I went to Japan in the winter, between the '78 and '79 seasons, I was presented with a Suzuki to test that, to me, had a host of glaring faults, the biggest being in the frame construction. I was far from happy with it. But the engineers insisted that Hartog and Ferrari were happy. Everything, they said, was in order with the modified bike and that was to be the model we were to race to try to regain the championship from Yamaha.

Their attitude hurt me and because I have always spoken my mind, no matter what the circumstances or who the people I'm dealing with, I pointed out a few facts of life. After all, I had ridden and developed the works Suzuki 500cc four-cylinder bikes from 1973. Originally they had been considered unrideable until I began winning Grands Prix on them. Did they assume that the bike was right on the impressions of two guys, no matter how good their racing ability, who had been riding factory Suzukis for such a short period of time? They were wrong, I said. The bike needed a lot of work and I told them I didn't want it until a variety of changes had been made.

'No, Barry san, no further changes. You must ride this one,' I was told quite firmly.

The first ride on the bike in 1979 was at the Venezuelan Grand Prix. I won it without too many problems with the opposition, but my earlier comments on the handling were confirmed.

The Japanese were all around me after the opening victory, 'Good bike now, Barry san?' they burbled.

'Are you mad?' I asked. 'It's diabolical!'

Hartog and Ferrari were rapidly beginning to change their

opinions. 'Doesn't handle so well, does it?' the pair remarked.

I quickly reminded everybody of what I had said in Japan and after a considerable delay a re-angled chassis was flown over to Europe. Not until the end of the season did the factory technicians acknowledge that my original appraisal of the bike had been correct and that alterations should have been made immediately. By then it was too late and the title had been retained by Kenny Roberts and Yamaha.

I had the distinct impression that we might have a repetition of the whole affair come the following winter's testing. Yet when in '79 Suzuki got around to constructing a frame embodying my suggested improvements, Hartog and Ferrari were given the revised chassis and I was left to muse over Suzuki's strange decision to leave me out in the cold. They clearly wanted to regain the championship and obviously regarded Ferrari and Hartog, in that order as better bets than me. On top of that came a rather nebulous suggestion that Ferrari was to be assisted in any way possible.

Now that was a problem. When we raced the Dutch TT at Assen in June '79, no indication of Suzuki's racing policy had been conveyed to me. That's if they had formulated a policy. Three laps before the end, after a battle royal between myself and Ferrari at the front of the field, I flashed past the pits and noticed that there appeared to be some kind of altercation over the board that is hung out every lap by my crew to inform me of my position and the gap between the riders in front and behind me. Knowing that a win for the curly-haired Italian could elevate him to the leadership in the world championship, ahead of Roberts, I had half expected some kind of chalked instructions on the board from the Suzuki top brass telling me to stay behind Ferrari. For the first time in my career I had been ordered to 'team ride'.

The Italian Nava Suzuki team had originally wanted my mechanics to show me the sign as I went through, but insulted by this request, they refused. But I was riding for Heron Suzuki. If there had been a pre-race meeting to thrash out a plan of attack involving the three Suzuki-importer camps, then I wouldn't have had to ride those last few laps in a state of total confusion. It seemed the Suzuki hierarchy had arrived at a decision during the course of the race. Possibly they had not anticipated that I would be a serious challenger after my run of misfortunes in the earlier part of the season.

What should I do? Seek personal glory by winning, or put the manufacturer's interest above everything else? Without any clear briefing from my employers, Heron Suzuki, I was left in a quandary. My mind was buzzing with permutations. As far as I was concerned, there would be little difficulty in beating Ferrari, but a victory might sabotage a possible over-all series win for Suzuki. That would really make me the bad boy in Suzuki's estimation.

The best approach, I reckoned, was to head Ferrari out of the last chicane and then wave him past. That would demon-strate to the packed stands that I was the moral victor, yet, at the same time, would satisfy Suzuki.

But Ferrari's desperate hunger to win, at what appeared to be any price, persuaded me to modify that plan. On a corner at the back of the snaking five-mile circuit, he really laid his machine on me and it was obvious I would be much safer tailing him, to avoid being dive-bombed again in his lust for the championship.

Ferrari reached the checkered flag first, a tenth of a second in front of me, to record a somewhat hollow success and, as soon as the garlanding ceremony was concluding, I tried to establish whether I should, in the future, race to win, or merely toe the company line. Clearly with Hartog, Ferrari and myself competing against one another, it made Roberts' life on the Yamaha that much easier.

I was contracted to Heron Suzuki, the UK importers of the marque. They were my paymasters and they expected me to win, or to do the best I could, wherever I raced, to attract the maximum publicity the massive investment in the racing effort by both Heron and sponsors Texaco warranted. Now it seemed that the parent Suzuki company in Japan wanted the British arm to act merely as a back-up to the Italian importer. The management at Heron were understandably miffed. (It was later interesting to learn that after my two world championship winning seasons, UK sales of Suzuki soared).

At a board meeting, straight after the Dutch GP, Heron

contacted me with their decision which was the one I had expected and hoped for: race to win and let Ferrari and company achieve their own results by themselves. Had they advised me to stay behind Ferrari in the future Grands Prix, I would have abided by their wishes. But executives like Gerald Ronson, Peter Agg and Maurice Knight didn't need reminding that outright victories by their rider would be infinitely more effective in boosting their marketing promotions within the United Kingdom than any achievements by a relatively obscure Continental rider.

Once I had received the message from the people who mattered most to me, I had absolutely no intention of easing off to allow Ferrari to gain an unfair advantage, even if it meant that Roberts and Yamaha would claim the title.

As if I hadn't had troubles enough during the last two years with Suzuki, I was struggling to get on with my official Texaco/Heron Suzuki team-mate, Pat Hennen, and made no secret of it. I could not forget his offering to take the place of my friend Gary Nixon in the Suzuki American team the moment Gary was injured testing in Japan. Hennen was quoted as saying he would ride for next to nothing and, I was told, he had suggested that Nixon might not ride again.

After Hennen badly injured himself riding in the Isle of Man TT, I had a new man in the team for the '79 season in the shape of Ulsterman Tom Herron. Now Tom, for so long the privateer, was once the most outspoken critic of me and the privileges I enjoyed. 'It's all right for you, having works bikes. You can't help but win,' he would say. We had argued a lot in the past and I can't say that we got on. When I heard that he had been chosen to partner me, I was convinced there was not the remotest possibility of our seeing eye to eye on anything. The atmosphere threatened to be unbearable.

But how wrong I was. His attitude impressed me right from the start. He was forthright and highly accurate with his criticisms of the way certain machines had been set up, a type of honesty which came as a refreshing change after having to listen to so much crap from others when they were asked for their assessments of machines. At last I had someone with me who would actually tell the technicians the way it really was.

The terrifying Silverstone crash. *Above* The bike on the track surrounded by the curious. *Below* Carting away the wreckage.

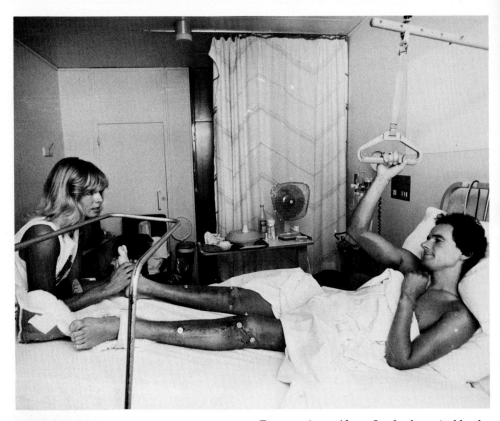

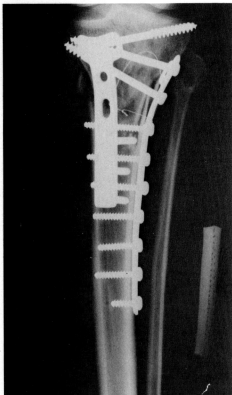

Recovering. *Above* In the hospital bed, Steph in attendance.
Below left The X-ray showing the engineering on my left leg.
Below right In my wheelchair.
Opposite Stepping out with Steph.

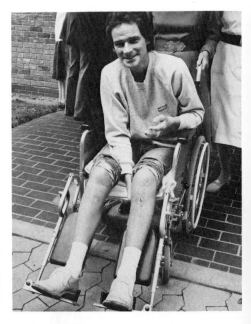

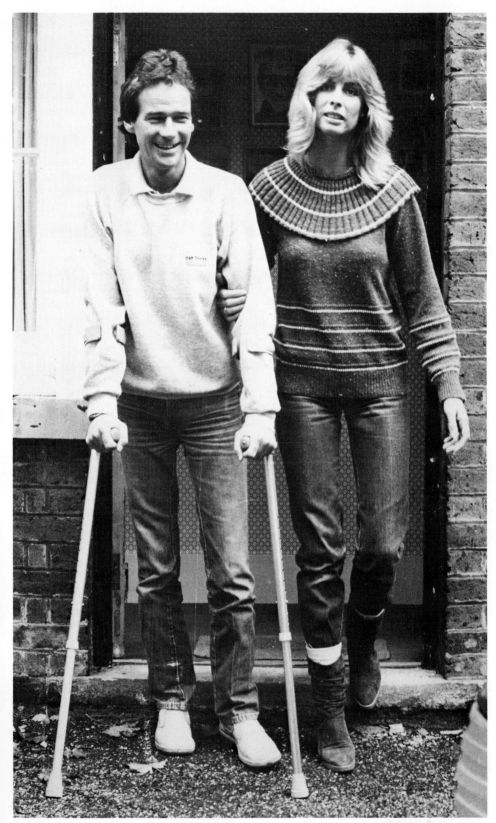

Above At Donington, on the road to recovery. Steve Parrish is the apprehensive passenger.
Right A souvenir – my Daytona leathers.
Opposite above With Steph and my parents.
Below left Our first public kiss.
Below right Togetherness!

Rewards. *Above* The house in Wisbech.
Right The animals.
Opposite above The Rolls.
Below Piloting the helicopter.

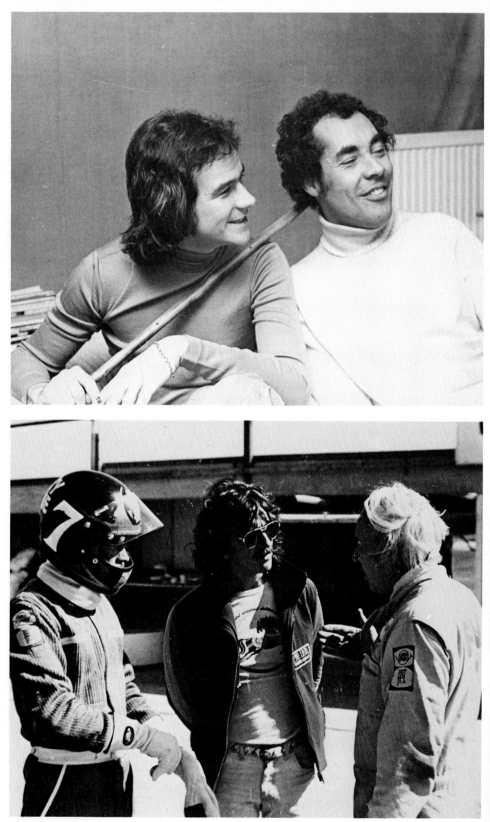

Opposite above With Piers Forrester.
Below With George Harrison and
John Surtees.
Above Cecotto, Parrish and me.
Below left Uncini.
Below right Graeme Crosby.

Opposite above Team-mates Tom Herron
and Steve Parrish.
Below With Mike Hailwood.
Above Agostini, Lucchinelli and Uncini.
Below Kenny Roberts – with a smile!

Preparation. *Opposite above* My own
patent weight training.
Below On the rowing machine.
Above The back protector.
Right Racing leathers.

Opposite With the 1977 Suzuki. *Above* on the starting grid.
Below Practice on the ill-fated V-4.

Above Some of my trophies. *Below* The future. Denys Rohan of Suzuki and me.

He never minced his words. Even if he thought I was a c***, which sometimes he did, he would tell me straight to my face. His direct approach was to be admired and, as far as I was concerned, I got on with him perfectly. If ever I was mistaken about someone, it was him. When he lost his life in the early summer, riding in the North-West 200cc meeting in Northern Ireland on the sort of closed-roads circuit he loved and supported, I lost far more than just a team-mate. I lost a friend.

I have only ridden in Ulster once, way back at the start of my career, but I have no yearning to try one of the province's 'real road' circuits which are supposed to enable a rider to prove he's a real man. Before he died on the Portrush-Port-stewart-Coleraine triangular circuit, Tom Herron reckoned I ought to inspect the place rather than base my opinion on hearsay. A consortium of local businessmen had offered me a big sum — well into five figures — to race there. But even if I didn't have other commitments, I wouldn't have gone. I'd heard about the fastest circuit in Europe from others who had raced there and lived to tell the tale, while the pictures I had seen confirmed my belief that it would be a place where I would not relish racing. It wasn't the 125 mph average lap speeds achieved on the 11-mile course that put me off going, nor was it the pressure of being expected to win there first time out. It was the vast number of hazards — kerbs, lamp-posts and brick walls — which added up to a circuit that could only be described as dangerous.

The start of what seemed to be my swansong season in Suzuki colours, saw me achieving my third successive win under the burning sun of San Carlos in Venezuela, sizzling conditions that suit me down to the ground. I was pleased to have the buffer of 15 points before Roberts — still recovering from a fall on the Yamaha test track in Japan — and his Yamaha returned to the world championship fray in the second round in Austria. But I wanted Roberts back on the track right away. If I had gone on to win a run of GPs in his absence some would have claimed that it was made easy for me. I wanted to win that title fair and square against Roberts. Never in my worst dreams could I have envisaged the disasters that lay ahead.

First, in Austria on the warming-up lap, I realised a mechanic had put an unnecessary washer behind the disc brake that had the effect of pushing the pads away. It was too late to remove it. It meant I had no front brake to speak of and even though Roberts lapped me, I kept circulating to try for a championship point. I managed only twelfth, two places out of the points.

Then in the West German round at Hockenheim the crankshaft broke when I was lying second.

In Italy, after a switch to Dunlop, the front tyre slithered about so much I considered that Michelin's development, no matter how slow, was worth sticking with. I came fourth, deeply concerned by the behaviour of the tyre. How would the Italian writers report that display? I wondered.

The Italian press have always been notorious for their tendency to publish anything remotely sensational, regardless of the sport, and when the 500cc Suzuki, in the early stages of its development, would constantly seize and throw me off, the Latin journalists would have a field day. My tumbles would always appear in photographs in the Italian magazines and they nicknamed me 'Crazy Horse'. As I suspected the reasons for my falls were being attributed to my riding techniques instead of the bike's weaknesses. I made a point of learning Italian to find out what they were writing about me. Command of the language also enabled me to phone one or two Italian publications to correct certain inaccuracies in their reporting of my crashes. Rider error didn't enter into it, I insisted.

(I picked up the language by making a concerted effort to listen to Italians speaking and also tuning in to the Italian service of Radio Luxembourg when I was touring abroad. Since I had a command of French and Spanish as well, I was in a much better position than most other riders to capitalise on the opportunities to be interviewed on television or radio at foreign Grands Prix where the interviewers spoke only their mother tongue. Now journalists speak to me in their own language when I visit their countries and so I stand an excellent chance of grabbing beneficial column inches in newspapers and magazines.)

At the next Grand Prix, at Jarama in Spain, the headlines were far from welcome. I crashed, hurting my elbow, in practice and was so demoralised when I couldn't start the Suzuki I felt sure there was little point in continuing once I had caught up the back markers.

The run of rotten luck culminated in the Yugoslavian GP with the strangest accident imaginable. I was following Marco Lucchinelli on the opening lap, when his knee, sticking out on a bend, touched the ground and flicked up a stone the size of a tennis ball which shot straight at my right knee, hitting one of the two screws inserted in the knee-cap operation four years before. It must have pushed the screw half an inch further into the bone. The pain was the worst I had ever experienced and for the first time in my life I cried with the agony as back at the pits, my mechanics lifted me off the Suzuki and laid me down on the tarmac.

But the Belgian Grand Prix, due to be staged on the newly constructed and shortened Francorchamps circuit, had to be regarded as the most significant meeting of the season, not because of the racing but because it saw the first real united front by the leading riders against a Grand Prix organiser. The track, slippery and oozing oil from the recently laid asphalt, was, in our opinion, unsafe to ride on. The FIM, following a series of rider representations, and a subsequent jury meeting, thought otherwise. That left those solo riders who were in contention for points no choice but leave the meeting the day before the race.

Work had begun in 1978 on shortening a track, clearly to encourage speeds which were beyond the control of many racers. I inspected the circuit a month before the 1979 GP when the surface was still uncompleted, but was reassured that all would be ready in time. The FIM were happy to pass it fit for racing though I understand homologation requirements do not include an analysis of the nature or condition of the racing surface.

Virginio Ferrari and myself, mindful of the many thousands who would turn up to watch, expecting a full grid of international riders, wanted the organisers to downgrade the

meeting to international status. Fewer risks would then have
to be taken compared to a fight for world championship
points, and at least the crowd would get something for their
money.

But the FIM, as archaic and uncaring a body as you could
wish to meet, were unbending. They wanted us to risk our
necks on a suspect surface which the tyres, at high speed,
could not adjust to. That danger factor had to be added to the
inherent risks of motorcycle racing, risks that tend to be
dismissed by certain factions.

A few did contest the GP, some doing a limited number of
laps to earn their start money and then returning to the pits
by way of protest, others to earn points from an event de-
nuded of quality riders.

This solidarity among the top names shocked the old guard
of the FIM; and we had a further surprise in store for them a
month later, with our announcement to the European press at
Silverstone of World Series, our own rider-organised championship that would have freed us of the present moral and
financial exploitation by GP organisers. It would be the last
year of competing in Grands Prix. But more about that later.

With Roberts regaining the lead in the championship after
Ferrari was unable to pick up any points whatever in the two
Scandinavian rounds, the situation over 'helping' my Suzuki
colleague became less of an issue. Pundits were already pro-
claiming a second successive Yamaha title, even though two
more rounds remained — Silverstone, and Le Mans, in
France.

I had won my fifth consecutive Swedish GP, on the Karl-
skoga circuit, and had ridden into third place at Imatra in
Finland with a huge chunk of rubber missing from my rear
slick.

The stage was set for what promised to be a classic British
GP — Roberts was on the verge of taking title number two,
Ferrari was anxious to bag maximum points and was hoping
for a Roberts breakdown and I was looking forward to finally
ending my run of below-par Silverstone results. Everything
pointed to the '79 meeting being a cracker.

All through practice from Silverstone the Suzuki was

handling badly. It was a pig to steer from the start of the week and only by trying everything in sight, did we begin to improve on qualifying times. Everything we did improved it — switching tyres, messing about with the forks, suspension and wheelbase — but nothing affected a cure. But by the end of the fourth timed practice on the Saturday afternoon, I was fifth fastest, far better than I had ever thought remotely possible. Yet Kenny Roberts and Johnny Cecotto on the works Yamahas were the quickest, on 1m 29.81 secs and 1m 30.72 secs respectively. Mine was 1m 31.35 secs — too great a gap for my liking.

Still far from satisfied once practice was over, I reckoned I had to attempt something drastic to get the suspension improved. I gambled on altering the damping characteristics. I had only the warming-up lap prior to the Sunday race to discover if this had done the trick. Once I returned to the grid at the end of the warm-up lap, I knew the adjustments had succeeded in making the bike handle a whole lot better. It was going like a dream.

Hartog led the way for about ten laps. Then Kenny went through; with me not too far behind him. Delighted that the bike was behaving so perfectly I found no great difficulty in holding onto Kenny and the pair of us rode side by side for many laps, as those who remember that great day will still recall. I was unconcerned about wanting some distance between me and Kenny; I figured I would make my final decisive and final move on the closing lap. I certainly had no intention of leaving it to the last corner, although I knew I was quicker going around Woodcote than Kenny. I merely wanted to stay within 25 or 30 feet of him until it was time to go, and I knew if I crossed the start and finish line on the final lap with only 20 feet separating his Yamaha from my Suzuki, then the race was mine.

Once we had dropped Hartog, Kenny and I were playing around, testing out one another's strengths but both of us aware, I think, that the whole race would hinge on the last lap.

We had been wagging our fingers and making friendly gestures at each other at various stage of the race as we passed

and re-passed; it injected a little light relief into our titanic
battle. The signs contained no malice. We were simply joking
with one another.

But as we rounded Woodcote to start the final lap, there
was the same guy we had already lapped, George Fogarty,
who had no business to be riding in the Grand Prix. Kenny
squeezed through on the inside of him but Fogarty drifted out
on me and the longer overtaking route made me lose 150
yards on Kenny. My plot had been blown by Fogarty's out-
ward drift, or so I thought. I did my best to recover the lost
ground and, as Woodcote loomed up, I was down by about
80 to 90 yards. I applied the power as quickly as I could going
into the fast right-hander but Kenny was hogging the tight inside line, forcing me to try on the outside.

As the finish line at Silverstone is still on the corner at the
exit of Woodcote, I knew I would have drastically to straigt-
en the bike up once I had got round Kenny. Reasonably confident I could still take him even though I had to go the long
way round, I aimed for an ever-diminishing hole betweem
the right track perimeter line and his Yamaha, that continued
to drift out as he stuffed on the power. Had I fancied there
was no chance of making up the leeway, I would have settled
for the safe second place and the accompanying 12 points.
But I just had to have a go. When Kenny went into Woodcote, I don't believe he knew I had pulled back so much
ground and he couldn't have noticed I was making a
challenge until I was right on his shoulder. As he had not
glanced back on the final lap to check the distance between
us, I figured there was a chance for me and so I picked the only available line which could take me past him. Had the
checkered flag been any further away, I might have squeezed
through, but at the end of the day, I had to settle for that .03
of a second deficit. My late burst had been half a wheel away
from success.

I was disappointed at the outcome, naturally , but I har-
boured no resentment against Fogarty. He didn't move out
on purpose, but the fact remains that riders of his calibre,
holiday racers, have no right to be given a ride in a Grand
Prix. They have one GP a year and start knowing full well

they will be lucky to escape being lapped at least once by the superior factory machines and by riders experienced in this type of racing.

Both Kenny and I enjoyed that race and were pleased that it might help boost the popularity of the sport to outsiders who had been unaware of how spectacular and exciting bike racing could be. They were the people that had to be impressed. And I guess the Silverstone crowd were pleased, judging by the way they poured onto the track on our winding-down lap. Everyone benefited from that race, and to produce good, close, exciting racing has to be the object of the exercise. We can do without boring, processional races, so often a feature of Formula One car events. I'll always make every effort to liven up what looks like being a dull race.

I understand that the crowd and everyone watching on television loved every minute of it. So did I, but there was no question of playing up to the gallery. As far as I was concerned, it was another head-to-head with Kenny which I intended to win. It didn't work out according to plan, but I wasn't that upset. There was always another time, another place.

The next 500cc Grand Prix in '79 after that epic duel was at Le Mans, where Kenny needed just a couple of points to secure the championship. The final round of the season, it was a repeat of Silverstone in some ways, with Kenny and I gesticulating at each other again. This time I got the break after Kenny had got himself mixed up in an accident involving my buddy from Venezuela, Roberto Pietri, and Gianni Rolando, a Grand Prix regular from Italy, and went off the road. I took the checkered flag first, with the front wheel pawing the air and, although it didn't register at the time, it was a fitting climax to my long run with Suzuki.

Some reports of that race suggested that Ferrari and I — he still had an outside chance of beating Roberts to the title if Kenny packed up and Virginio finished first in this GP — were banging into each other in the early part of the race and were said to be 'stealing each other's lines'. That wasn't exactly true. I never steal anyone's line. Ferrari was riding like an idiot and I had no intention of getting involved with him. Neither was I going to allow him to hold first place.

He went off the track on the eleventh lap, returned to the fray, tried to ride round Johnny Cecotto on the outside and crashed into the catch fencing, the bike, apparently, landing on him. He had tried to lay his bike into Cecotto's Yamaha when they were cornering but Johnny refused to give way. So Ferrari only had himself to blame.

Early on, he banged so hard into me I couldn't believe someone of his calibre should be riding like a lunatic. He rode like a fool and ended the race the way he deserved to. Thankfully, his injuries were none too serious.

It was another really good race and I had to consider myself fortunate that at the hairpin I got through on the inside of the melee involving Pietri and Rolando while Roberts didn't. Without that incident, he, Randy Mamola or myself could have taken the race in the last section.

The folks at Le Mans appreciate a big wheelie so I gave them a special on the main straight. There's no great science involved in riding on the rear wheel. Roll on the power, give the bars a slight tug and, as long as the bike's revving within its power band, the front end will come up. You then just regulate the throttle to ensure you don't flip it over backwards. I always think the wheelie adds a final flourish to winning a race, provided there's sufficient breathing space between you and the next guy. In many respects, it's like the victory roll of the fighter pilots in the last war. You do it to acknowledge the cheers of the crowd and as a means of displaying your own personal satisfaction.

In spite of a splendid series of results in the remaining five GPs — two firsts, a second and a third — the problems of the first half of the season had ruined the challenge and I had to console myself with third place, two behind runner-up Virginio Ferrari.

But I'll remember that French GP as much for the night before the event as for the actual race. As I do every time I'm at Le Mans, I was staying in an elegant, five-star hotel in the town and went to bed feeling really tired at around 11 o'clock, only to be woken two hours later by what must have been the loudest band in the whole of France. The noise from the dining room below was so great the bottles in the refrigerator began to shake and rattle. I couldn't believe a band could produce such a volume of noise and so I phoned down to the manager to express my feelings. Had we been forewarned there was going to be a late-night dance, Steph and I might have joined them early on or booked into another hotel but I hadn't anticipated that commotion from such a high-class establishment at that time in the morning.

In my initial rage when it was apparent the noise was not going to subside, I emptied the contents of the bottles in the fridge over the balcony of my first floor room. The splashing had no effect. By this time, windows were opening everywhere and people all over the place were appealing for peace and quiet. Still no change — the band played on as enthusiastically as before. That did it. I gave the manager another warning that I would do something drastic unless he took immediate action. He didn't. So I unplugged the 26-inch colour television, carried it to the French windows and pushed it over the edge. When it hit the courtyard, the tube exploded with an enormous bang. Bits flew everywhere. Thirty seconds later, the last notes of the tune they were playing died away and I went back to bed in perfect silence.

Next morning when Steph realised what I had done she became somewhat concerned.

'You'll be in trouble now,' she said, looking down at the debris, an assortment of electrical components, glass and pieces of cabinet. I couldn't possibly have raced the next day if I was dead tired. I could have lost my own life or taken someone else's because I was dozing off.

'The police will lock you up,' she insisted.

'I don't care.' I said, remembering that I had also threatened the manager that I would smash up the room before descending to do the same to him.

When I came downstairs the next morning for breakfast, I can distinctly recall seeing the manager slink away as I appeared. Although Steph continued to talk about the dire consequences that awaited me, I figured all would be forgotten when we returned to the hotel that evening. After all, I had been a welcome guest at this establishment on many occasions in the past.

Sure enough, when we got back that night, there stood a new television in the corner and an ice bucket on the table containing two bottles of champagne. Attached was a note from the management apologising for their 'mistake' the previous night and stating that it wouldn't happen again. Apparently it was the first time they had held a dance there — and it would be the last.

I've never reacted like that before as it takes something really serious to make me angry. But when I do lose my temper, I mean business, like the time when I had to wring an apology out of a gang of yobs who were kicking my Rolls Royce, and another occasion when a guy refused to pay my father a debt outstanding on a bike and I had to resort to physical violence to extract a promise of money.

But it wasn't anger that led me to think about my future during the autumn of '79. More a feeling of sadness, really. Looking back over the previous two seasons, there had been numerous headaches — true, some problems had been ironed out, but others remained. The future with Suzuki seemed uncertain.

The virus trouble was the first omen of disharmony. But once I was fit again the results began to go my way and it proved I hadn't been pulling the wool over people's eyes. It had been genuine sickness that left me weak and helpless. Yet I believe the factory remained unconvinced. Then the business the following year over the deficiencies of the new bikes remained a bone of contention with the technicians. They wouldn't accept my judgement despite the fact that I had been instrumental in helping to perfect the 500cc racer through all those years.

If only they had listened to me, instead of relying on the instant diagnosis of others. That mistrust did nothing to help rebuild what had once been a good working relationship.

I knew it was time for a change. I was no longer happy riding in such an atmosphere and so a split had to be made. It would be wrong, I considered, to race for Suzuki under the mistaken impression that everything in the garden was coming up roses. The mood was simply not right. It was the end of the road as far as I was concerned. I attended what would normally have been the annual end-of-season contract talks with Heron Suzuki at their Croydon headquarters and immediately told them, 'I no longer feel I want to ride for you.'

Back in '75 when Suzuki Japan decided to pull out of direct involvement in bike racing, I would have negotiated a fresh contract with a different manufacturer had not Peter Agg and Maurice Knight of Suzuki GB pleaded with the Japanese to supply them with the machines to set up a Grand Prix team stable in Britain. The British Suzuki distributors agreed to put up the money needed to race in the world championships.

From then on, they were happy to pay me what I considered to be a reasonable salary, negotiable every year, but allowing for a decent increase annually. Many people speculated about what Heron Suzuki were paying me and all I will say is that it was the going rate for the job. Any suggestion — and there have been many — that it was around £100,000 at its peak are completely wrong. It was far lower than that. I had quite a number of team-mates during those four years, but though I still like to think I was the highest paid of them all for the effort I had put in and the results I achieved, I never enquired about their retainers. It didn't interest me.

During my long association with Suzuki, not once was I approached by, or asked to have end-of-season talks with, any other Japanese manufacturers. It would not have made much difference if they had attempted to woo me with amazing new machines and large contracts, because I was happy with the Suzuki set-up and, up until 1979, always rated the RG500 as a strong contender for the world title in spite of Yamaha's domination under Roberts. Nor did I make personal representations to Yamaha to suggest I was available during my final unhappy year as a Suzuki rider.

Heron Suzuki had supported me since 1976 and I felt duty-bound to honour any contract I had with them. I never once became involved in the crazy, year-end, rider merry-go-round. After the considerable time I had spent with the Japanese developing the 500, I could not envisage life without being part of a Team Suzuki of some description.

But events don't always turn out as planned. I went into that meeting with the racing director of Heron Suzuki,

Maurice Knight, as a full works rider with all the attendant backing and came out of his office with absolutely nothing — no bikes, no contract and no income whatsoever.

From my association with Suzuki, I took only a store of memories and a more permanent reminder in the shape of the two championship-winning 500cc machines and the 1979 bike. They are on display at the Donington Collection in Derbyshire where circuit owner Tom Wheatcroft, or 'Wheatie' as we call him, has amassed an entire museum of prize bikes and cars.

Now I started to rethink my life. Perhaps four wheels might be an answer. Cars have always interested me and there was a time when they could have ruled my life. When I was still employed by Suzuki, I made my first serious moves to try my luck at car racing. Support for me came from many quarters and I felt I ought to find out if I had the necessary skills. The original plan was to enter the Aurora series for Formula One cars on British circuits in an Arrow, to serve a twelve month apprenticeship. A secondary plan of mine was to combine both sports. Suzuki and I reached agreement and my contract was rewritten to allow me to race both cars and bikes in '79.

I went ahead with the scheme not knowing whether I was good enough to compete at that level or even if I would enjoy it as much as running bikes. My confidence was boosted by my first outing in a racing car, when John Surtees allowed me to drive one of his Formula One TS19 outfits on a mid-week test session at Brands Hatch. My lap progress showed I was not too far away from a good time which suggested to John that possibly I had what was needed to make a success. I managed to cruise within 2.9 seconds of the lap record after 70 laps. It was no major problem to achieve the fast time, but the experience, although enjoyable and requiring immense concentration, did not stimulate me to the point where I felt I just had to switch to four wheels.

In the end it was money that stymied my plans; not the lack of it but the conflict of interest between the firms prepared to put up the £300,000 that was required. Two sponsors were happy to back me in a car, but unfortunately, they produced the same kind of electrical components. Reduced to half the necessary finance, my dreams of racing cars evaporated. Looking back, I suppose I am glad it worked out that way, because now I believe it would have been a total mistake to have switched from motorbikes. Being heavily involved with the preparation of my bikes, I realise there would be so much to learn about the pre-race setting-up of the car. A lot of my satisfaction comes from locating a specific mechanical problem and offering advice that will eradicate the trouble. I would have wanted to apply the same approach to cars although it would have been a long time before I could have felt confident of my ability to do so.

In 1980 I had my last competitive drive. I went in for the BMW County saloon car championship, driving for Akai in a dealer-entered fuel-injection BMW323. Gordon Provan of Akai telephoned me a week after I had smashed my little finger at Paul Ricard to see if I was interested in contesting a round of the series at Ingistone near Edinburgh.

The BMW had a race-tuned engine, trick suspension and slick tyres, altogether a very neat motor car. Practice went well and I grabbed pole position a second and a half ahead of some highly-respected drivers. The race went even better and I won by about eight seconds.

But when I passed that checkered flag, my car racing career was over. While it was mildly enjoyable, I knew in my heart that the world of bikes was where I really belonged. I am a motorcycle racer and cars are not for me.

To start learning a fresh trade at the age of 28 would have been a mistake. The best age to make the transition would have been about 22. It wouldn't have been the right thing to have done, yet if the adequate financial back-up had materialised, I'm sure I would have gone for it. It's a blessing, I believe, that the sponsorship failed to work out.

So it was back to bikes, and that meant Yamaha. It has to be said that Yamaha machinery was the only option to me. Honda were in trouble with their NR500 four-stroke project which never seemed likely to succeed and Kawasaki were only on the fringe of 500cc GP racing at the time. The Yamaha 750 had shown it could win races and with one of those I fan-

cied I could pick up some useful results in internationals in
the U.K. The 500cc standard production bike may not have
been the bee's knees, I thought, but in time, improvements
would take place. The early teething trouble could be sorted
out and I was reasonably happy to take the chance.

My heart was set on running my own team. Financially, I
would get a better return from my racing and, most important of all, I would be in an ideal position to control my own
destiny. I would be in charge of everything, wallowing in
satisfaction when races were won and accepting total respon-
sibility when things went wrong. At last I would be able to
decide the way I wanted work done, which mechanics should
do it and what meeting I wanted to attend. I could be my own
boss.

On paper, it sounded perfect. But, of course, it could never
become reality without one key item: money, and a great
deal of it. To pay for the four bikes — two 500s and two 750s
— plus all the tackle, transporter, mechanics' wages, running
and travel costs demanded a colossal sum. Anything I hoped
to make out of the sport would have to come from race win-
nings and start-money fees. All the other bills would clearly
consume any sponsorship cash I might obtain.

Contrary to popular belief I had no giant multi-national
conglomerate waiting in the wings ready to hand me a blank
cheque. No time had been spent warming up potential sponsors before my departure from Suzuki. All I could count on,
or so I hoped, was the goodwill of certain contacts I had
established over the years.

Akai and their UK chief Gordon Proran had been pleased
with the coverage they received when I had raced at Ingistone
for them. Now I felt it was time to translate the relationship
we started then into a useful alliance. Nothing else had happened between Akai and myself for several weeks but I
thought I would repay their kindness at the big Race of the
Year meeting which, this time, was being held at Oulton Park
in Cheshire. This event which died in '81, ranked among the
more prestigious British race meetings. I had won there
several times before, and was desperately keen to put on a
good show. Knowing the race would be televised, I stripped

an Akai sticker right across my helmet. I fancied the cameras might zoom in on me because of the vast amount of padding and plaster around my shoulder, the legacy of that week's instant operation. There were no deals agreed with Akai, I merely wanted to do the company a favour and I guess they must have been pleased by the amount of exposure their name received from my second-placed ride.

Aside from a class entry to contend with, I had the added problem of riding with a collar-bone strapped up. At the previous week's meeting, at Imola in Italy — the AGV Nations Cup — Franco Uncini on the 650 Suzuki crashed into the fibre-glass kerb at the chicane and a portion of the edging was knocked out into the middle of the track. I had no chance of avoiding the obstacle. Off I came, straight over the handlebars, fracturing my collar-bone. Two days after returning home from Italy, I flew to Brussels to have the damage repaired by a Belgian surgeon, Johan Derweduwen, known for the quality of his work and his ability to get broken motorcyclists quickly back into action. Never mind the discomfort, I just couldn't bear to miss the Race of the Year only 120 hours away and I was fairly sure the plates and screws holding the collar-bone together would not restrict my movements too much once I was in the saddle.

When it came to chasing up possible leads, then, Akai topped my list of potential backers. The Japanese parent company were mounting a major sales campaign in the worldwide hi-fi and video markets and the British end needed a promotional effort to capture greater brand awareness. My promotional agents, Championship Sporting Specialists, soon made contact and it didn't take long to form an alliance.

Akai was to be my main supporter and the bikes and transporter were painted in their colours, black and red. Texaco and Marlboro also came in with me to complete the £250,000 package I required, the largest sponsorship arrangement motorcycle racing has ever known.

I still like to believe the two years spent with my three sponsors were good ones, with everyone getting what they hoped for from their involvement. I don't think I gave them cause for complaint. Even though I went through a fairly traumatic season in 1980, Akai had no qualms over renewing the tie-up for a further twelve months. Then because of a decline in the hi-fi market, they withdrew from all forms of sponsorship. Texaco simply pulled out of all motorsport activities, while Marlboro and I failed to come to terms over a new deal.

People thought I must have been crazy to switch from factory bikes to standard production Yamaha machinery in 1980. But I was doing what promised to make me happy. Above all, I had formed my own team.

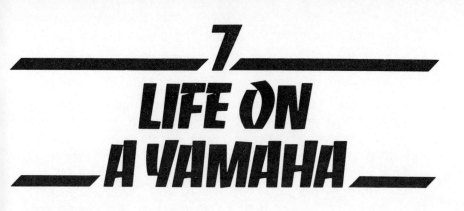

7
LIFE ON
A YAMAHA

Clumps of golden daffodils, always a feature at Cadwell Park, nodded in the April breeze as I methodically blipped the throttle of my Yamaha as the seconds ticked away to the start of my first race as a privateer for nine years.

The traditional opening British international meeting of the season had pulled in a huge crowd, well in excess of 30,000, with many travelling to that hilly north-eastern part of Lincolnshire to see if the Sheene magic still existed, now that works machinery no longer cushioned me from my rivals.

Many of the enthusiasts craning their necks to get a glimpse of the red and black Team Akai with Texaco machine must have considered me stupid to turn my back on works-supported bikes which guaranteed a regular salary come rain or shine, in order to ride on standard production racers that were relatively untried and which anyone could purchase.

But numerous high placings with a variety of riders on board had confirmed that the 750 Yamaha was capable of winning races. A quick survey of results indicated it would always earn its keep if ridden properly.

The fact has to be faced, though, that the 500cc bike, the one I would contest the world championships on, was regarded as an unknown quantity because Yamaha had not previously sold these over the counter. But I was content to soldier on for this one 1980 season in the hope something good might materialise. The skill in riding a racing motorbike does not vanish overnight and I felt confident that races could be won on the 500 if it was up to anything. There would, I knew, be teething troubles but I began the campaign in the right mood ready to bypass whatever difficulties came along.

The struggle to win the world title for Yamaha in the face of opposition from Kenny Roberts and his full factory backing made life even tougher and I realised the Suzukis I had left behind were still potential race winners at the highest level.

That day's racing at Cadwell dispelled an awful lot of doubt amongst my fans. My will to win, as strong as ever, took me to first place in the two big events and everyone around me seemed to be smiling. The Cockney flier was back!

When I assembled my new team, I wanted to launch it with a bit of style. That would demonstrate to international sponsors that they could get considerable publicity mileage for motorcycling. The massive chunk of television and radio time devoted to what was the biggest-ever bike racing launch in Britain must have pleased them.

A touch of distinction was added to the lavish proceedings at the Royal Garden Hotel in Kensington by the 'round-table' interview on my racing programme by Frank Bough. It was no coincidence that the BBC celebrity had the same marketing agency as mine!

Running my own team soon had me involved in long and heated discussions with certain race promoters. Chris Lowe, the supremo for Motor Circuit Developments, was one. As he was responsible, until the end of '82, for negotiating all start money arrangements, we clashed head on while trying to reach an amicable financial deal.

He laid his cards on the table by offering me £40,000 to ride at six of his international meetings in Britain that year, including his company's biggest money-spinner, the Transatlantic Trophy, in which a British team annually took on the visiting Americans. I was keen to contest all those meetings but, knowing crowds might top 100,000 for the three-match Easter series and realising the vast amount of money MCD would make, the terms I was seeking for the Transatlantic Trophy were more than fair, taking into account the huge outlay necessary to run the team over a season.

The previous year I really earned the £7,500 Chris Lowe paid me for three events at the Race of the Year, since I had spent £5,000 on the collar-bone operation in Belgium so as

not to let anyone down. Roberts was paid £11,000 for just
one race at that same meeting I understand, but what he received did not worry me. I merely wanted adequate compen-
sation for the job. With no agreement in sight I was all set to
race abroad that Easter Bank Holiday at Paul Ricard in
France if agreement could not be reached over what had become a matter of principle. I spent little time wondering if all
this would harm my image. I believed, rightly or wrongly,
that most fans were on my side.

At the eleventh hour, Chris and I sorted out our money dif-
ferences and I competed against the United States team, although none too brilliantly. After the opening rounds at
Brands Hatch, where I rode well, the 750cc Yamaha kept seizing because, we later discovered, the oil we used was unsuitable.

When the Grand Prix season dawned in Italy, it was soon evi-
dent private machinery was no match whatsoever against
works tackle. The days when a privateer could win the big
prizes just about came to an end in '79. The different manufacturers place so much significance on winning the world
championship that the tempo of development in the various
Japanese race shops increase daily. On top of that, I was
slowly trying to learn how to handle a bike with monoshock
suspension, which required a skill all of its own. It demanded
a different approach because of the way the power was applied, hence changing the handling.

I was the leading non-works rider in the world championship chase, and although my results were poor I never once
questioned my own ability as I struggled. You can fool
anyone but yourself and I knew in my heart I was riding OK.
It was simply that the bike was just not good enough in such
rarefied company.

Even when Yamaha supplied me with a special engine and
a works rolling chassis for the British round at Silverstone
that year, matters didn't improve. The bike went slower and
slower in the race until I realised there was little point in
continuing unless I wanted to finish last.

Chris Lowe, courteous to a fault, once again had serious

discussions with me over contractual arrangements for that season's Race of the Year. Astute businessman that he was, he held out to the very end before improving his offer and I rode, finishing ten seconds behind Randy Mamola after my Yamaha developed a fault.

At the garlanding ceremony afterwards when Fred Clarke, the commentator, asked me what problems, if any, I had experienced during the race, I replied the bike was plagued with a misfire. I gave him a truthful answer but certain sections of the crown groaned, assuming it was another Sheene excuse.

I had realised long ago that some cynics refused to accept there could be genuine mechanical reasons for not winning races but I was never one to offer replies to questions that merely contained the kind of statements the crowd wanted to hear. I would tell them what really happened and, if they were disinclined to accept the truth, that would be entirely up to them.

At Oulton Park an effigy of me dangling from a hangman's noose was erected by some complaining spectators, obviously incensed by the amount I was being paid to entertain them. Slogans were daubed on the Mallory Park track which screamed 'Sheene—rip-off'. Everyone's entitled to their own opinion in a democratic society.

Mamola, the young-looking American, was by then making his mark. But I could never understand why he hardly ever smiled after winning a race. There wasn't a hint of happiness on his freckled face whenever he headed the field home, which was strange, as he was riding well and deserved his success. What would happen, I said to Steph, when his form slumped and he had to struggle to make the rostrum week after week? The '82 season supplied the answer. He was the picture of misery as one disaster followed another. But he possessed the strength of character to bounce back and, once he began winning again, he finally shook off the attitude that he was invincible — a feeling which plagued his 1980 season.

At the tail end of the '71 season, I had begun to feel that coming first was my entitlement every time I wheeled the Suzuki out. The next season soon brought me down to earth with a considerable bump when nothing went right. That served as a timely reminder that rewards only come as a result of considerable hard work and dedication. I thought I was the best thing since sliced bread but I was quickly taught a lesson. Randy had to learn this same lesson.

If ever a guy was misunderstood it was Randy. He's easy to get on with and will offer definite views to those who are prepared to stop and listen. The commonly-held notion that he lacks any kind of personality and would make the most boring champion the sport has ever experienced is simply mistaken. People's judgement has been clouded by his manager Jim Doyle, whose outspoken remarks would often be attributed to Randy. If someone put a question to Randy, Jim Doyle would pipe up and answer it before Randy could open his mouth.

Whenever I'm asked to isolate the worst crash from the many I've been involved in I've no hesitation in naming a really bad one which was, in my view, much worse than the Daytona and Silverstone prangs. It was at the Paul Ricard circuit during the 1980 French Grand Prix, when I foolishly allowed myself to ride with my heart instead of my head.

With my Yamaha nowhere near as competitive as the factory bikes, I considered I was doing well to hang onto fifth place. Graeme Crosby on the works Suzuki was racing with me and, on the straights, he would zap past me, his machine developing an extra 15 mph above mine. Through the chicane at the end of the Mistral straight and on to the start and finish section, I could make up lost ground. But it was really tough going and with the front tyre pattering more and more with each lap through deficient fork damping, the job grew harder by the minute.

What I should have done was to settle for a safe eighth or ninth and err on the side of caution. But I didn't. I kept trying and trying and it wasn't long before the pattering increased to such an extent it took the front end away on a left-hand bend. From that position there is no recovery. The front wheel must have been off the ground because of the pattering and when I touched the brakes, the whole lot went smack on the floor.

With my normal hand position on the bars, two fingers are ready on the clutch lever in anticipation of the dreaded engine seizure. This leaves my little finger hooked around the rubber grip of the handlebars. Even now you can never take a two-stroke motor for granted and it's always wise to be ready to react in the event of a possible seizure. If it misses a single beat, you jerk that clutch lever in. So when the bike went down so quickly, the knuckle of the smallest finger was immediately trapped between the bars and the road with the finger locked in its normal position, around the rubber grip.

After somersaulting several times and ending up on the grass, I could feel blinding pain coming from my left hand and I looked at it to see the finger hanging down through the disintegrated leather of my glove, amidst pieces of smashed knuckle bone. Not a pretty sight!

The medical team at the circuit flew me to the local hospital where they wanted to amputate the finger without delay. I turned down that suggestion rapidly and had them repack, as best they could, what was left. As soon as I arrived in England, I visited Donald Brookes at the University College Hospital in London who attempted to put it together. But without the knuckle, the finger refused to move and was therefore useless. The top half might as well be removed, I thought. Fortunately, the reduced finger has made no difference to gripping the bars. The one disadvantage is apparent as I rinse my face after shaving. When I scoop up the water from the sink with my hands together, the water escapes though the gap where the rest of my finger should be!

A pin had been inserted like a skewer down the centre of the finger, to give it strength, but it slipped out a little way during the Dutch TT when I accelerated hard out of a corner. The wrench from the bars did the damage. When I pushed the pin back, I must have allowed some dirt to get into the wound and by the Belgian Grand Prix the following week, the finger had turned septic. The agony was so intense I had to quit the meeting to come home after practice, in which my disability had helped keep me way, way down the list of qualifying times. Then came the operation to amputate the finger.

It ranked as my worst spill because it eventually led to the loss of half the finger, the only occasion when I have had to sacrifice part of my body. Although it's no handicap to me whatsoever, I feel upset that racing has taken away a small part of me, through my own stupidity.

Although I was always confident in my own ability, from the outset the 1980 season was basically intended to be a suck-it-and-see effort.

One way or another, it was a difficult year and I realised my 1980 performances might not have been regarded by the Japanese as dramatic, to say the least. Still, I was far from being disenchanted, even after what had to be described as my blackest year.

The big chance to impress the Yamaha supremos came with an invitation to race at Sugo in Japan where I knew an impressive display in front of the attentive Yamaha VIPs might tip the scales in my favour so far as landing a factory contract for '81 was concerned.

The most pleasing aspect of the race was that almost all of us were to ride the following year's production Yamaha racer which meant the only advantage would be superior rider skill. With Kenny prohibited from running his works machine, this was the real test, I thought. All the bikes would be on a par. It was so nice to sit on the line aware we were all equal. If you were no good, you would not get in the first twenty.

Run over two legs, the first race saw me leading by some distance before the machine seized and put me out. Then in the second race, I held an identical ten second lead when, on the last of 60 laps, the front tyre punctured and I was thrown off into the Armco barrier. The track was covered in water from the incessant rain as I went into a right-hander. The tyre deflated as the machine was doing something in the region of 130 mph. The front end slid away and I bounced across the track backwards. Hurtling towards the barrier, I instinctively shot out my hands to protect my head. As I lay there with a broken wrist, one of the first faces to peer down at me to enquire about my state of health was, in fact, the president of the Yamaha company, a man I had previously met at the FIM Congress in Venezuela.

At the local hospital in Sugo, I refused anaesthetic when the medical team came to set the wrist because I wanted to catch an early plane home. An overnight stay in hosiptal would have interfered with my plans. So they held me down, muffled my cries of anguish and expertly reshaped the wrist. I rate that experience as the most painful I have ever had to endure.

Back home again, I had my usual London surgeon Donald Brookes put a cast over the injured wrist that would leave the hand in the right position to grip the bars of the bike which I had planned to ride in the final Brands Hatch meeting of the season. In his surgery I held the handlebars I had brought with me, and he applied the perfect plaster mould.

A condition of Yamaha supplying me with factory machines was that I must agree to follow team instructions. If Kenny Roberts was out in front of the world championship table and he needed my help to stave off the opposition from Suzuki, I would carry out orders to achieve outright success for the manufacturers. If the situation was reversed, I could also expect support from Kenny. This brought back memories!

The only regrettable aspect of the deal-clinching ride in Japan was that the Sugo race was the last opportunity I had from Yamaha to race on equal machines. After that, I was always one step behind Kenny in getting the lastest machines.

I received my first factory bike — designed for Kenny — halfway through '81. For the round of the world championships in '82 in Argentina, Kenny had had three weeks of testing there which gave him a useful advantage over me. I was told that the machine was practically unchanged from the previous year's model but it turned out that it sported cylinders of a different specification which provided an extra six to seven horsepower. By the Austrian GP, he had the new Yamaha V-4 which I didn't have a chance to ride until the ill-fated Silverstone week. Ironically, although I had the inferior bike at that Austrian round, I knew I could have beaten him had not a stone been sucked into the carburettor, seizing the motor, while I was leading.

It had to be said that Mitsui, the British Yamaha importers, and the European headquarters of Yamaha Amsterdam did everything in their power to get me the best possible bikes. But they were always thwarted by the inconsistent attitudes of the racing department at the Yamaha factory.

Whether their decision to give me only second best had anything to do with the strained relationship between me and Yamaha back in 1972, when I was one of four riders — with Jarno Saarinen, Rodney Gould and Chas Mortimer — to receive factory support from Yamaha in the 250cc world championship, I'm not quite sure. That was a trying year, fraught with arguments and disputes and perhaps I was more critical of their machines than a person of my age and experience should have been. From the word go I maintained that their new dream bike, a water-cooled twin, was useless.

It was nowhere near as quick as my standard air-cooled Yamaha which I took to the French GP at Clermont Ferrand. There I qualified fastest but was told by Yamaha I couldn't race it. I had believed that the object of the exercise was to win races for Yamaha. Instead, the engineers were far more concerned to develop this water-cooled machine.

Fair enough. But what I had set my heart on was the new 500cc racer Yamaha were shortly due to unveil of which I had only seen pictures. Finn Jarno Saarinen and Hideo Kanaya from Japan were to race this new machine and I couldn't disagree with Yamaha's choice. Both were good runners, Jarno being prehaps the most brilliant rider around at the time. I was promised that I would have the 500 half-way through the year, but I was desperately keen to move into the big class where all the excitement seemed to be generated. So when the chance to graduate up the scale came with Suzuki, I accepted with relish.

My fault in '72 was that my comments — usually critical — on the machines should have been directed to one person such as the chief engineer instead of to the public at large.

One or two members of their racing department seem to carry a chip on their shoulder and I would be a liar if I said otherwise. It was noticeable, but it is hard to pinpoint the precise cause. But I'm old enough and wise enough now to know the best thing to do is to ignore those who hold a grudge against me.

The terms of the Yamaha agreement for '81 were, I was led to understand, that I would be given exactly the same kind of machines as Kenny would have. But that promise was a sham from the start. I began the campaign with an '80 model racer with the four engine cylinders stretched across the frame.

Kenny, always one jump ahead, was presented with the newly-designed square four — on which he won the Grands Prix in West Germany and in Italy — and this left me struggling to hold on until I received the potent racer at the the French round.

With a fourth place in Austria, a sixth in Germany and a third at Monza in Italy, I was doing all I could to score points within the limitations of the machine. The difference once I got going on the square four was immediately apparent — it had more power all the way through the range, which made it an infinitely preferable machine to the virtually obsolete model I had previously been racing. But tyre troubles were to be the undoing, both of my machine and Kenny's, at the French meeting.

We were using a 16-inch front wheel which appeared to offer good stability but still the tyres were a problem, as often was the case. I had used Dunlops once or twice after my Daytona crash when I felt the Michelin tyres were unsuitable in certain conditions. I might have done so in the French round, but Dunlop had sufficient 16-inch tyres only to cover the needs of their contracted riders and the Suzuki works runners, Mamola and Crosby. As I felt I would be at a small disadvantage using an 18-inch front rim, I had little option but to use a Michelin in the race.

For a circuit like Paul Ricard where speeds of up to 180mph along the Mistral Straight are possible with 500's, and many of the fast corners test adhesion to the limit, correct choice of tyre is critical. Remember that the bikes are leaning over 45 degrees from the vertical and yet we expect to use most of the machine's 130 horsepower. The tyres are also asked to withstand incredible braking forces that seem to want to tear the rubber apart. So the tyre designer has to produce a product which offers the right balance, by matching different constructions and various compounds, taking into consideration track surfaces (Ricard is slippery these days), the bike's power characteristics, its weight distribution, riders, personal preferences, and atmospheric temperature. What a daunting task!

Practice went OK. I was third fastest and confident I could show everyone a clean pair of heels. During the initial stages of the 21-lap race, Kenny and I traded places at the front and began to build up a lead on the rest. But then my rear tyre began to slide about, as did Kenny's, and the handicap was almost impossible to overcome. This time, the Michelin seemed unable to come to terms with the Yamaha's mono-shock suspension arrangement and, although I attempted to make a fight of it with Mamola and Crosby, I had to be satisfied with fourth, about half a second behind Randy who was second to Marco Lucchinelli.

All the same that debut on the rotary-valve square four drove home to me how superior it was in terms of power. Tyres and their durability were clearly going to be a problem and the handling required fairly urgent attention, but here was the basis for a winning machine. I realised then what I had been up against.

A new frame, made to Kenny's specifications, was quickly constructed by Yamaha in Japan and rushed to Rijeka for the Yugoslavian Grand Prix. An identical one was also intended for me, but it didn't take much of the early practice session to convince me that the handling problem had become even worse now the engine was rehoused in the changed chassis. The only way we could make it rideable was to take out the old frame and modify it ourselves. While that made the bike behave far more reasonably, a catalogue of disasters checked any progress I hoped to make. Dutch — couldn't start; Belgian — clutch failure on lap one; Silverstone — brought off; Finland — broken power valve.

Only in the San Marino GP at Imola, where I came second to Lucchinelli—that year's eventual champion—and in Sweden, where I won in the wet after qualifying as fastest in the dry — did anything pleasing happen in the big events.

That left me fourth overall in the championship which was something of a failure in my book. Number one spot is the only place to be. Champions are the only guys remembered.

In the Yugoslavian round, where I came fifth on the wiggling Yamaha, we had to kick up a fuss over a problem that was to recur with serious consequences, the following year, on a circuit closer to home. A guy had crashed on the Rijeka track and there was no sign of any marshals at that particular point to give some kind of warning to following riders. I led the move to have the number of flag marshals substantially increased and also to have a few more ambulances standing by. The organisers carried out our wishes — and we raced happy in the knowledge that precautions had been taken which could possibly help to save the life of some unfortunate who happened to lose control of his motorbike.

My performances, however, were good enough for the Japanese to instruct the UK importers, Mitsui, to take me on again in '82 and to pay me a salary I considered fair.

When I discussed my new contract with the Yamaha officials at the end of '81 I was again given no indication that I would be treated any differently to Kenny. When I tied up a couple of big international wins after competing at the Sugo event, I figured the late burst might have eliminated any misgivings they might have had about my deserving equality in terms of machines.

For the Malaysian Grand Prix, an event that carries a considerable amount of prestige in the Far East. I had a particularly tough schedule. First, I had to jet to London from Tokyo, where I had been testing tyres. Then I had to catch a connecting flight to Madrid to race at Jarama where I won. Airborne once again, I flew on to Singapore via Heathrow, then to Kuala Lumpur for a 3 a.m. arrival. By 10 a.m. I was testing the bikes, which were running well enough for me to win both races in the non-championship Malaysian GP, blowing off Randy in front of the massed Suzuki officials who wanted their man Mamola to boost their export drive in this part of the world.

In '82, after Akai pulled out of the sport, I had others keen to back me, who were prepared to put up the same amount of finance as John Player. But Player's had indicated that they would up the ante in 1983 which made me feel they were the ones to go with. We were looking for £400,000 and their executives, aware of this figure, made no discouraging noises during the discussions.

What made me delay announcing my '82 team sponsors until so late in the day was the withdrawal of a consortium of Middle East businessmen, who were unable to give me a positive decision in the time that remained. In the end I had to plump for Player's at the last minute.

They should have been delighted at the way the season of '82 began to shape up.

After claiming second place in Argentina, I was all set to win the opening European round at the Salzburgring, in Austria, when dirt in a carburettor caused one of the pistons to be almost burned through, incredibly without seizing the engine, which made the bike falter on uphill sections. Still, that second place earned me a rostrum berth — two in a row. I was beginning to enjoy being back amongst the champagne once more.

Oozing confidence that early summer despite the knowledge that Kenny Roberts' superior V-4 could thwart my efforts, I motored over to Nogaro in the south — west corner of France for the next stage of the classics. But once again the whiff of rebellion was in the air and I had no hesitation in joining forces with my colleagues in the riders' revolt. Nogaro had always been a dumb choice as a circuit on which to run a Grand Prix. With two good circuits in Ricard and Le Mans it made little sense to choose this Mickey Mouse track as a venue, especially as it lay, literally, in the middle of nowhere.

There were two main reasons for the majority of the top riders departing well before race day. Most importantly, the track surface was so bumpy that it was only suitable for moto-cross events. It was almost unrideable. Then the paddock, where every square inch was taken up by transporters and mobile homes, presented an obvious fire risk. A blaze could quickly have got out of control and swept through the whole paddock with horrifying conseqences. We left with threats of fines and withdrawal of licences from the FIM hanging over us once again.

I have never paid a fine to the FIM nor worried about possible action against me. I simply concentrated my thoughts on the task of collecting vital points. Spain gave me 12; Italy none, thanks to the ignition packing up.

Holland should have yielded me more than the ten I achieved. Torrential rain halted the race when I was leading. When the conditions were considered suitable for racing and we re-started, I again headed the pack by about four seconds, only to get into a dreadful slide which loosened my grip on the bars. My arm smashed the perspex screen on the fairing and the bars were so twisted by my effords to correct the skid, I could barely turn right. I managed third.

At Francorchamps for the next round, Freddie Spencer and his Honda-3 had the inspired day they had always promised to have, although the British fans in the large Belgian crowd will agree that I was pegging back his narrow lead. A further 12 points in the bag.

Honda's latest weapon impressed me. The three-cylinder motor with reed valve inlet seemed to kick out a lot of power and looked as if it handled as well as the manufacturers intended. That's unusual in racing. During the winter of '81, I would often talk well into the night to Marco Lucchinelli who had just been testing the new Honda after switching from Suzuki. He praised the Honda's amazing speed, and bubbled with enthusiasm in the way only Italians can.

Doing my duty to my masters, I rang the chief engineer at Yamaha in Japan to advise him to the rapid progress Honda had obviously made. By all accounts, they had produced a machine that would pose another threat to Yamaha's desperate bid to win the championship.

'Look, a Honda, I understand, is developing really well. We should be doing something to make sure we're not going to be blown off,' I insisted.

'That's ridiculous,' he replied. 'Our reports say it's a hopeless machine.

But consistently high placings and some rapid lap times made the Japanese top brass at Yamaha take this new threat more seriously. Having ridden against the three Hondas in '82 I don't doubt the machine is capable of taking the title, with Spencer likely to be the man to help them to do it.

Although they are the biggest motorcycling operation in the world, I have never had talks with Honda about riding for them. Nor have I ever wanted to. Riders who bob from one factory to the next seem to lose credibility in the eyes of the public. I made my major change in 1979 and that was about the final move I intended making.

The last stop before the vital Silverstone race, where I was banking on a maximum return, was at Rijeka and the 10 points for third spot left me ready to strike at Uncini's top of the table position. The scene was set for a trial of strength in the Northamptonshire countryside.

We all know what happened next.

8
STYLE OF A HERO

My build-up to a big race, once the anxieties of practice are over, begins with a very low key and relaxed evening at a nearby hotel where I'll have dinner with close friends before retiring to bed at a reasonable hour.

Now I'm one of those who has never regarded sex the night before as being taboo. Sap your strength? What nonsense! I believe making love is an activity that cannot be restricted by timetables. Do it whenever you and your partner feel like it, is my attitude. If that means love sessions on the morning of a race, I've no objection. I have never felt it has impaired my stamina when riding a motorbike later in the day.

Some racing drivers I know have said that sex before a race is the ideal way to release tension. But, when I go to bed, there isn't a thought in my head about the next day's sport. There's no tension to lose. All I want to do is drop off into blissful sleep, or do whatever comes up.

Whenever I race, I always stay overnight in a hotel, in order to ensure a good night's sleep and to get away from the pressures of the paddock. I stopped sleeping in the rear of transit vans and in cramped caravans in the early seventies, when I realised that the extra cost of a hotel was money well spent. Ever woken up on a freezing cold morning after spending the night on the floor of a van, competing for bed space with spare wheels, oil cans and tools? Droplets of moisture would cover the inner walls of the vehicle and you would climb out of a damp sleeping bag knowing the first race would be the rush across the paddock to beat everyone else to the normally appalling washing and toilet facilities. So, before anyone complains I've never experienced the hard times, let me say I have worked myself into a position where I can afford hotels and can see the benefit of using that kind of accommodation in preference to my 30-foot motorhome. The motorhome is merely used as a paddock base and is fully equipped right down to a coffee grinder and had to be worth the £28,000 outlay, even though it only does 9 mpg.

I'm never really keen to spend the whole day at the circuit. You need time to yourself and being kept awake late by the commotion of late-night parties, and woken early by revving bikes, as happens in the paddock, isn't the best preparation for a race.

Once I open my eyes on race day, I push back the covers and tear the curtains apart. Shafts of sunlight filtering into the hotel room bring a smile to my lips; if the skies are leaden and the windowpane is patterned with rivulets of rainwater, I know I'll need extra time at the circuit to organise wet-weather tyres and to change the carburation.

But it's important to line the stomach, no matter how pressing the need is to get to the track. Stamina has to be maintained and so I'll fuel the boiler with eggs, bacon, toast or whatever is available. A round of sandwiches at mid-day, washed down with tea, will be the only additional intake before the race.

Best not to take too much liquid aboard, I've found, because the pre-race build-up can bring on a pressing need to visit the toilets at the very last minute. In the '80 French GP at Paul Ricard, they were so long in releasing riders onto the track, I was dying to spend a penny. Propping the bike against the perimeter fence, I rushed to a tunnel in front of the grandstand, the nearest thing to privacy, and had to relieve myself.

That would seem to be the closest I get to suffering from nerves on the day of the race. I'm so busily engaged in machine preparation there seems little time to worry about what might or might not happen during the race. My composure in the countdown has to be the result of years of experience. I stopped feeling over-awed by the occasion, long

long ago when I set off on the Grand Prix trail with a few pounds in my pocket and a burning desire to be the best-known racer in the world.

The nearest I get to being affected by an attack of jitters are the odd occasions when I've become so immersed in making intricate changes to the bike that I have tended to shut myself off from everything else and to ignore anyone who might distract me.

'Hey, Barry, I'd like to talk to you for a few minutes,' is a common enough question on the morning of a race as someone creeps under the awning, brushing past the beavering mechanics.

'Please, not now — my racing matters most of all at this moment and I just don't want to be disturbed,' I will reply, perhaps wondering afterwards if I had been misunderstood. Too bad. Number one priority is always to ensure the machines are properly set up for the task that lies ahead. To allow anything to stand between you and achieving that perfection has to be a matter of life or death.

Immediately after the obligatory warming-up lap before a Grand Prix, for my own peace of mind I let one of my team hold the machine while I dismount to give it a quick checkover, with the front tyre having priority. I always like to ensure, if it's a new slick, that the shine has gone and it is ready to do its job. It's no use discovering that it has not been sufficiently scrubbed in on the first corner, when you're left on your backside.

Removal of the glossy rubber surface can begin in the pits. Often my guys rub the slicks beforehand with acetone or emery cloth, a roughening-up process to help make the tyre sticky when the temperature of the compound is raised as the bike squirts along the straights.

For most races, I would start with a new back tyre. There's no need to run the rear beforehand because it is comparatively easy to control a rear wheel slide. But a front end slide can be almost impossible to correct and so I might scrub in the front tyre over a few laps in a practice session, although I prefer to break in a fresh tyre on the front on the warm-up lap when I'll lay the machine over as far as possible each way to remove all traces of shine. I happen to believe a tyre that is allowed to cool once it has reached its operative temperature does not perform so adequately afterwards.

It's a fact of life that the results of many of today's races are decided by the quality and durability of the tyres. Choosing the correct compound for the race can often mean the difference between winning and coming in well down the order. What I hope is that we have reached the limit of tyre development. We most certainly do not want tyre technicians to develop tyres as they have for Formula One cars, where the tyres are so big as to be ridiculous. There must one day be a limit introduced to the size of tyres, although the basic theory that the greater the area of rubber on the ground the greater the grip will always apply. But still you come up against all kinds of variables over whether or not the profile and the compound are right for the job in hand.

There is a universal problem in that some tyres are not compatible with certain track surfaces. On very smooth surfaces, such as at Imatra in Finland, the tyre has great difficulty in being 'roughed up' to its working temperature and consequently big lumps of rubber can come off the slick.

A slick can also become 'greased-up' after the rubber temperature has fallen below the optimum level, which makes it slide violently.

But a slick has to be the safest racing tyre devised. The movement of the thread of a patterned tyre is increased when it becomes hotter and thus significantly increases the chances of the tread being torn apart. There is nothing worse than to go out on a dry surface with grooved tyres on a 500cc machine. It makes the bike wobble to an alarming extent. Ten years ago, when speeds were much lower, and technology was less advanced, the patterned tyre was suitable in the dry. Not now.

I believe I was among the first, if not the first, to race a 500 on slicks in the Belgian GP in '74. They were put on my bike as part of Dunlop's early experimental work with this new kind of tyre. I wasn't sure what to make of it at first. There were no grooves to give the bike traction and it didn't occur to me that the less grooves there were the more rubber there was on the road to give better grip.

Now people often moan at me because I have an advantage over those who have to pay £70 for a new tyre of standard construction because a factory contract with Michelin means that I can have mine made to order, compliments of the manufacturer. I too had to buy tyres, of course, when I first started. There was no fairy godmother. But perseverance and the enthusiasm to do well will bring their own rewards — which could even include a contract with a tyre company.

The warming-up lap's main purpose is to allow the rider the chance to ensure that his bike is running correctly and that there is nothing substantially wrong; a shake-down of the bike, really. To suppose that it is simply a means of bringing the tyres up to their optimum working temperature, as many race commentators have suggested, is untrue. By the time you're back on the grid and one delay follows another before the actual start, a lot of the heat has left the tyre. Since I prefer not to really buzz the engine, the real benefit from that first warming-up lap is to fluff up new slicks to remove that gloss and to bed in new brake pads.

My worst memory of a warming-up lap comes from the Salzburgring, prior to the '79 GP, when I came to an uncertain halt on the grid, after circulating once, to discover that the front brake was not functioning. A mechanic had put together the front disc brake assembly with a washer behind one of the discs. This left the disc out of true and it kept knocking the brake pads out of line. Of course, there was nothing that could be done in the time available and I had to struggle through the race relying on the rear disc only, something used just to stabilise the machine on certain corners. I might have squeezed into the points that afternoon, but two rivals outbraked me in that their machines had stopping power!

Another time at Chimay in Belgium, the sidewall of the front tyre collapsed on the warming-up lap and we just had sufficient time to slot in a fresh wheel which should take a capable mechanic around a minute (rear wheels take a little longer).

Carburation can prove troublesome and, in my first year on a Yamaha factory bike, I recommended to Yamaha they put on a central choke lever to eliminate the hassle of having to operate four individual choke levers, each attached to a carburettor, by hand.

'No, that would be add too much weight. We want to keep the weight low on the bike,' I was told.

'Well if I eat a hearty English breakfast with four rashers of bacon, six eggs and so on, that will weigh more that a choke lever. And what's the point of having a light bike if you cannot get it off the line?' I responded, after weak carburation was found to be the reason for my failure to get the Yamaha started after desperately pushing the bike away at the start of the '81 Dutch TT. The works Yamahas now have choke levers fitted as standard.

When the board which indicates that there are ten seconds remaining is displayed, or the middle amber light beams out from the starting lights, my visor is securely fastened with gentle pressure on the push-studs on either side of the helmet.

If there is a suspicion of drizzle in the air, I will run a finger over the tape masking the gap between the top of my Bell visor and the AGV helmet to ensure no water drips will creep on to the inside.

As many road riders are aware, the visor on a full-face integral helmet can become steamed up occasionally and so I always try to eliminate this problem by coating it with Fairy Liquid washing-up detergent. If water does work its way in, however, the subsequent suds give me trouble.

What also helps to prevent misting-up is the placing of a strip of duct tape over the bottom of my nose to funnel hot air downwards rather than on to the visor.

If it's a brilliantly sunny day, I'll wear one of the tinted visors the Government's trying its best to abolish. They serve a useful purpose when glare hampers your sight. If it's raining, a quick wipe with rubber gloves, which don't carry any grease, will clear rain droplets that might be obscuring my vision. Riding at less than the ton, there is little danger in removing one hand from the bars. But at speed, I'll merely turn my head sideways. Water that has collected on the visor will immediately blow off.

To guard against the risk of flies and insects splattering across the visor and masking my view, I have a couple of rip-off plastic visors. But nine times out of ten, I don't bother to tear them off, though they're handy if you get a big custard-pie fly spread itself right across your sight line.

Right from the beginning of my racing career, I've sported a Donald Duck painting on the front of my helmet. What began as a joke became an instantly recognisable trademark. The Walt Disney character, I reckoned, reflected my initial happy-go-lucky approach as well as giving me a certain identity.

The sight of pictures of my first year's racing when I wore the ancient 'bone-dome' style of helmet makes me feel quite old. That was all I could afford in those days. Then, after riding with an open-face Bell Star, I joined the first wave of racers to go for the American full-face lid which had to represent the safest form of head protecton invented. Many others were to follow my example of having my name written across the rear of my helmet, which enabled me at the time to stand out from the crop of up-and-coming riders.

The wearing of all-white leathers, as opposed to the conventional black suits, was also a deliberate move to make me easier to spot. Rod Scyvyer led the drift to leathers of a brighter colour but I began to feel my whites were a little over the top. They didn't seem right on me, too gaudy by far, and so I discarded them after one season.

I like to secure a grid position on the first couple of rows. Fast practice times are valuable for establishing one's capabilities compared to other riders. It does help to obtain a front row grid position, though I'm not disappointed to have to start on the second row, as long as I'm toward the inside of the track to minimise the chances of some joker torpedoing me from behind. The front row allows an unimpeded passage. What I try to avoid like the plague is to get caught in the middle of the pack at the first corner; I aim to keep on the inside so that I won't be scooped up if a rider falls off.

There's little to choose between electric light and the traditional flag method for starting. With lights, it pays to watch the earlier races to determine the time gap between the 'get ready' amber light and the green for 'go'. It can vary from circuit to circuit but at least the lights can frustrate those who attempt to jump the start, a trick which annoys me as much as anything. I don't cheat and I don't expect others to.

Certain starters have particular mannerisms that give an indication when they would raise the flag to release the pack. Others jitter with the flag and seem to take pleasure in reforming the grid as riders inch forward. In the big Italian meetings, you can count on the starter giving his idol Marco Lucchinelli a big wink to let him know he was a split second away from starting the race.

If I'm lined up next to a rider known to appreciate some quickfire banter on the grid, I'll chat to my neighbour. Lucchinelli and Boet van Dulmen, the placid Dutchman, almost expect some conversation, while others, slightly nervous and constantly fiddling with the bike's controls, prefer to be left alone in their private world. If you can see someone is visibly nervous with eyes the size of dinner plates, there's no point in adding to his misery by fooling about with him on the start line. There are riders who will be so twitchy, they're rocking their bikes to and fro when there is still at least a minute to go before the off.

Knowing what some of those within the FIM think of me, I deliberately keep the machine two feet back from the white grid marker line so they can find no excuse to bust me. Once the command to go is given, I try to restrict the pushing of the machine to three or four paces before dropping the clutch and firing it up by banging my chest on the fuel tank. If the carburation is perfectly set up, it should immediately burst into life. The 1982 GPs I contested were super in that respect as I was the first away from the line every time. There have been races where it hasn't chimed in, but in that case I'm too busy pushing and wondering why it hasn't started to worry about the rest shooting by me.

As soon as the engine fires, I pull in the clutch, rev it round to the red mark at 11,000 rpm and swing my right leg over the back. I'm away. With one eye on the rev counter and the other on the road ahead, I'll be cautiously slipping the clutch to feed in and control the necessary power. Once in the saddle, my legs will be outstretched, the soles of my boots skimming the track as a precaution against the bike pivoting over backwards if a king-size wheelie catches me unawares. By the time both wheels are together on the ground, it'll be time to change into second gear.

At the first corner, I've an eye on the hero trying to sneak up on the inside line who may be the one who could bring you down. The bloke in front has to be watched like a hawk, too, if you're in the middle of a 40-strong pack. If he falls down, there has to be an escape route mapped out on the inside of him.

Redgate, the first sweeping, right-hand corner at Donington Park, is the most notorious obstacle in Britain these days. If I'm leading the field away at the start, that suits me fine. But if I'm amongst the heavy traffic going into Redgate, count on me coming out towards the back. It's that nerve-wracking. The race allows plenty of scope for making up time — but not if you're lying in the back of an ambulance.

Race tactics, as far as I'm concerned, don't really exist and I hardly ever spend time beforehand figuring out what my race strategy is going to be. Only in the thick of the action can a clear picture form of where certain riders in front demonstrate weaknesses and you learn to remember the sections where they can be taken. It's just a matter of commonsense.

I ride the race as it comes, with the object of getting under the checkered flag first. Second place is of no interest to me. Winning, with the minimum of effort, has to be the goal.

I like to give a competitor ahead of me a couple of mock overtaking moments just to deceive him into thinking I'm preparing to pass at that part of the circuit as the race nears its climax. However, I'll perhaps save my overtaking manoeuvre for somewhere else, at a point where I've made him feel he can master me because he thinks I can't take that section as quickly as he could. What I try to avoid, especially in a home international where the standard of opposition is less severe, is rocketing out in front and staying there to the finish. That makes for boring racing which the public would quickly tire of. And it's hardly fun for me, wandering around on my own.

Slipstreaming can play a vital role. The advantage from a 'tow' can be enough to win a race and so it is most important to try to shake off someone using you like that. His slipstreaming, of course, also helps to slow you down, so a guy out in front can widen the gap between him and a pursuing pack of riders slipstreaming one another.

Although the rev counter offers a constant reminder of the engine's behaviour, a trained ear will be able to detect when it's time to change gear, or if anything is amiss with the power plant. Good hearing should also pick out the engine note of another machine on your tail without having to look round. On a sunny day, the shadow of a chasing bike will also be apparent.

I have to admit my hearing has been impaired working amidst the noise of motorbikes. Years ago, I should have worn earplugs which would have left me with normal hearing. It began to go about ten years ago and now, if I'm in the middle of a noisy bar, I may have to struggle to hear a conversation. Doctors have explained that the damage has been done through working constantly in a noisy environment. In my opinion, the best thing that ever happened in racing was the introduction of silencers which brought the noise down to a more tolerable level. In the days when I raced with the legendary MV Agustas, the sound may have been music to the ears of the spectators but, to me, it was bad news. Slipstreaming Phil Read and Franco Bonera, both on the MV's, at Francorchamps for almost the whole of a Belgian GP left me with the most intense pain in my ears. I could literally feel the resonance coming from those MV pipes as it damaged my ear drums, in spite of pushing my head from one side to another.

Where I need to get by on a bend, I can brake as late as anyone and later than most. Going into corners, I tend to brake early, which means I travel around the corner faster and am left in a position to get the power on quicker.

A lot of people have commented on my extravagant use of my knees when cornering, a style favoured by most of today's top racers. I ride like that because it feels comfortable and I find it's the riding position that suits me best. But what may seem on the face of it an almost ugly and ungainly pose to adopt is, in fact, an ideal way to get the bike around corners in the most successful fashion. This hang-off style has been part of my riding since I first started. The knee and shin scrape the tarmac and the backside is right out of the saddle. I can't imagine racing any other way.

Back in the old days, riding 750s, the semi-hazardous act of applying maximum power coming out of corners had a tendency to spit a rider off and so it was advisable to keep as much tyre as possible on the track. Tyre development for motorcycles was very much in its infancy in the early seventies; certainly it was not progressing then at the rate it has been from 1980 onwards. So the rider had to lean off the 750 as far as he dared in an effort to keep the machine as upright as he could to keep the largest area of tyre rubber in contact with the ground.

My brother-in-law, Paul Smart, was noted for his exaggerated habit of virtually separating himself from his 750 at corners in the formative years of superbike riding, and although I rode in this fashion on most categories of bike, I recognised the even greater value of hanging off with the 750's.

As I crank the bike over, the unwelcome thought of leaning the machine past the point of no return never crops up. If something does begin to scrape the ground, you just hang off a little more to ensure the bike can assume a position nearer the vertical. To use a more scientific explanation of that cornering style, hanging out helps to balance the G-forces and to lower the centre of gravity. My style feels right but I dare say the riders who prefer to remain in the saddle with knees tucked in are equally content to ride that way. It's a matter of doing what feels right. I find that going into a corner, the leg seems to be forced out naturally when the machine is laid over, a reacton effected by the forces of gravity.

The knee often rubs along the ground on bends but, with nylon knee pads backed by foam rubber and covered by duct tape, there is normally little chance of harm. One advantage of the knee trailing the track is that it can act as a prop if the back wheel decides to hop out. That happened at Imola once when a new Dunlop tyre gave way for no reason at all. With my knee protruding right out, it assumed the role of a training wheel on a kid's pushbike and the stabilising effect stopped the machine from toppling over.

What you have to watch out for are objects on the perimeter of bends such as kerbs which give the unwary a nasty crack. But if you feel you're trying to squeeze in too close between a kerb and a rider in front, it's no major effort to swing the leg back into the fairing.

Whereas the earlier Suzuki models would once, when fully cranked over, scrape the road at the base of the fairing, today's machines are designed with everything tucked in to allow sufficient ground clearance at any angle of lean, even with the suspension under full compression. This still doesn't prevent some riders from grinding away the outer toe section of their leather boots on fast bends. I'm not amongst them because I ride with my toes on the foot-rests.

Keen observers of our profession have suggested that I have a fondness for racing in the wet and that a downpour gives me an advantage over those who don't like wet conditions. That's not strictly true. Like most others, I dislike riding in the rain and it's usually the ruin of a good race. But I ride to the same limits regardless of whether the track conditions are good or bad.

In a race on a dry surface, I very rarely slide the machine. I am rarely forced to tackle a big slide through over-enthusiasm. I try really hard not to get into sliding situations through going beyond my own safety limits. Nor do I bounce off kerbs in chicanes where I can help it.

Riding in the wet requires an even more precise approach. On a sodden and slippery track, once you have committed yourself to a definite line or a passing manoeuvre, there is little chance to alter your decision by applying the brakes, by giving the throttle a big handful, or by cranking the bike over a few more degrees. The consequences of doing that at speed on a damp corner are fairly obvious. So you do sensible things.

There is no possibility of throwing the bike about in the same style as in the dry and those who regularly perform below their best in wet conditions are invariably riders who have experienced a bad moment in the past when, more than likely, they have been tossed down the tarmac through racing too exuberantly in the prevailing conditions.

Take the Dutch TT at Assen in '82. When the heavens opened up and it bucketed down, Roberts came flying past me with slick tyres on his Yamaha. The track was covered in water and I thought, 'Oh God, he'll have fun.' Up to the next corner and, sure enough, there was Kenny in a heap on the grass after the slicks had aquaplaned him out of business.

I wasn't prepared, and never will be, to take those kind of risks. Self-preservation is the name of the business and, when the weather's bad, you ride with a wide safety margin between you and disaster.

And it's untrue I rub my hands with glee if it starts to rain before a race. As long as my bike is on par with my rivals, I want blue skies overhead and a bone dry road underneath. The only time I'm happier when it's pouring is when I have to race a machine that is clearly uncompetitive compared to those of the other front runners. Then I know a wet track will neutralise their advantage because of my ability to master it.

The discomfort of wet riding is known to everyone who has taken out a bike on public roads during a shower. Enduring that unpleasantness at racing speed is infinitely worse. It's a totally miserable experience, I can tell you. A nylon oversuit should prevent water from saturating your leathers, but try getting one to fit properly. If they don't billow out, rainwater often trickles inside at some point, normally along a seam. It wasn't until I began wearing a Finnish Rukka oversuit that I finally found a garment of this type that satisfied me. My only other change for wet riding is to slip a pair of household rubber gloves over my normal racing gloves: perfect protection against having wet and cold hands, and the hands have got to be cared for above all else if I am to maintain full control of the machine.

But normally in a race in the rain, you are left to face the elements in your leathers. It doesn't take long before water starts to creep down your neck, your thighs are soaked and your bottom feels extremely damp. But provided your concentration on the road ahead is total, it takes a lot to be detuned by the wretched conditions.

The cold is the aspect of racing I enjoy least. That's why I often wear a white polo-neck jumper under my leathers to keep out the draughts or else stick a newspaper on my chest to combat the windchill.

The race that I reckon had to be classed as the one run in the most diabolical conditions, had to be the '78 British Grand Prix at Silverstone, when it poured and poured soon after the start and made any kind of racing practically impossible. Some bikes were equipped with full wet tyres, others had intermediates on and many poor so-and-sos, like myself, were on slicks.

It was complete chaos from the word go and must rank as the only Grand Prix in motorcycling history where no-one — and I'm positive that included the official lap scorers — had any inkling whatsover of who had won or how the points-winning positions were filled.

When I pulled in, wet, cold and feeling about as miserable as was humanly possible, five Italians sprinted up to me yelling, 'There's no way Roberts could have won! Lucchinelli must have won.' Others nominated different riders whom they thought had triumphed but nobody I met reckoned Roberts was the rightful winner.

I hadn't a clue where I had finished. My pit-lane board had long been put away that afternoon because my chalkers were, like everyone else, completely in the dark over race positions.

My one pit-stop to change from slicks to full wet tyres after stupidly trying to circulate in the rain shattered any ambitions of mine. There was no sense in running a slick when there were oceans of surface water about. But my crew were in total disarray. The Suzuki mechanics were simply unable to locate where they had placed their kit containing the tools needed to change the wheels. I sat on the pit wall for minutes having a cigarette while they panicked like headless chickens searching for the spanners. Far from being annoyed about the lack of professionalism, I had to smile to myself. Where was all this Japanese discipline?

Kenny's team, on the other hand, had planned Silverstone perfectly. When it began to pour with rain and the water lay inches deep at certain sections, Yamaha team boss Ken Carruthers signalled to Kenny to come in to change tyres as soon as they saw me pulling off to do likewise.

He had his wheels changed in 2 minutes 28 seconds; mine took 7 minutes 31 seconds. It wouldn't be an over-statement to suggest that that margin of deficit was just about impossible to make up in those conditions which I, and most of the 60,000 spectators, thought were bad enough to have the race stopped. I had my feet down at certain corners and went at walking pace through other sections. Commonsense ought to have prevailed, but the organisers deemed racing possible. They should have been out there. I would have loved to have had one on the back of the bike to see how he would have got on. If that had been a Formula One car race, the red flags to stop racing would have shot out as soon as the first drops fell, and those vehicles offer some protection to the driver, unlike bikes. The driver won't go skidding down the road as we can.

I went back out to circulate as quickly as I dared as many times as I could before the bloke with the checkered flag appeared to send everyone in. It was no longer a race, merely a survival exercise to see who could keep going at a respectable pace. Some of the riders had correctly chosen to race with intermediate tyres on from the start and those were the ones who had no cause to waste time in the pits.

Well before any race, I make a decision over which type of tyre to use and there won't be any last-second wheel changing on the grid. That time I had gone for slicks because I felt the rain would hold off and when this kind of tyre works up its operative temperature, making it nice and sticky, I would say it's worth at least a four-second advantage over intermediates.

After the tyres had been changed in my record-breaking

pit-stop, they say I was lapping five seconds quicker than anyone else. All I could do, not knowing where I lay in the race, was to pick off as many riders as possible in the time available and hope the officials could sort it all out. But I wasn't blind to the fact that Kenny's pit stop was a swift affair by comparison. He pulled in the same time as I did and I was still there when he departed.

In the confusion afterwards, one thing was clear — I knew I hadn't won and if the dozens of other viewpoints were to be believed, Kenny hadn't either. Lucchinelli had not stopped for a tyre change and he had been travelling quite quickly in the wet, considering his Suzuki was shod with slicks. So perhaps he really was the winner and not Roberts. We may never know.

Kenny, of course, has been in racing long enough to know how to ride safely and to inspire the confidence of those who happen to be dicing with him. He is excellent to race with in close proximity, because you know full well he is not going to do something foolish like shoot up the inside or slam the door on you as you attempt to get past. Freddie Spencer is in the same commendable mould. But regrettably there are riders, top level competitors, who are so unpredictable it makes racing with them a lottery. One American in particular left behind some bad memories. They will lean on you and block your free passage. These tactics are all pathetic in my opinion, ones I would never want to adopt.

People have said that Kenny is no longer hungry for success after winning his three world titles, but I don't necessarily believe it. What I do believe is that Spencer is the American at the top of the tree and I don't think that can have a beneficial effect on Kenny. Spencer is the faster man of the two and, to my mind has definite world championship potential.

Once the race is over, a check of the tyres is imperative. Could we have done better with a softer compound? Why did it slide? Have they shown any sign of wear? That information, along with my own comments, will be given to the tyre technicians and the data processed back at headquarters.

These details will also be logged by my chief mechanic who keeps a huge book containing every modification we make to the bike — sprocket sizes, plug gaps, tyre compounds, gear ratios, jetting, suspension sizes, wind speed, even the weather and humidity. Every detail at each circuit is recorded for future reference.

Mostly I can dig into my memory bank and remember the changes we made to a machine to tailor it to the demands of the track. That helps to keep the mechanics on their toes if they become too complacent to check their official monitoring register. But the hand-picked squad I have chosen to look after my machines command respect. They wouldn't be with me if they were not up to scratch, and they know full well they wouldn't be asked to do something I am unable to do myself.

For no other reason than for the sheer pleasure it brings, my first priority upon dumping the bike in the pits is to have a cigarette. I might have had my last drag on the start line but I crave one immediately I've finished the race, not as a means of calming the nerves but simply because it has been over an hour since my last one. For a heavy smoker like myself, that's a long time!

Then, if I've been fortunate, it's a bee-line to the award presentations...

9
WHAT THE
FUTURE HOLDS

From the evidence of a career stretching back to '67, I see little prospect of development within the sport of motorcycle racing. That is my honest opinion.

What will prevent any growth in the forseeable future is the stubborn, blinkered, selfish attitude of the hierarchy, the allegedly wise men who feel ordained to preside over what should be a most progressive, professional sport. If motorcycle racing has made any strides forward in the past ten years it is in spite and not because of the ruling authorities.

I have never been afraid to express my opinions publicly. Speaking on behalf of the other riders to the FIM, the all-powerful body whose inflexibility on matters relating to improving the riders' lot is legend, presented few problems for me. As the riders' elected spokesman, I tried to do as much as I could to make the FIM face reality over track safety and over the relationship between fair pay and the risks involved. The first rider to speak at a general council meeting, I said at the time I thought I'd get a reputation as an international stirrer. That might have been the case had I been allowed to continue to act in that capacity.

In the two years I was the riders' representative to the FIM, I saw all I needed to confirm all the doubts I and many others felt about the way they control our sport. You could talk to them at council meetings until you were blue in the face, but still they would not listen. They seemed to have made up their minds on every issue, however burning, before you even had an opportunity to express the views of the riders. When they did listen, it was only out of courtesy.

So it was no great hardship when I lost the backing of the British federation, the ACU, as riders' representative to the

FIM. Comments of mine in the press constantly appeared to antagonise the ACU in general, and their chairman Vernon Cooper in particular. But my remarks, honest and constructive, were an attempt to ensure that my collegues made the controlling authorities aware that we felt justified in demanding a fair deal for the job we had to do. I was disappointed that the ACU could not keep faith in me, but hardly surprised.

When Mick Grant was nominated by the ACU as FIM rider representative on the grounds, according to Vernon Cooper, that 'he was a better committee man', I was annoyed, because this move was made without anyone bothering to inform me. What annoyed me most was a quote from Cooper denying suggestions in the Press that the proposed ACU changes were due to animosity between us. After all we hardly ever saw eye to eye.

The first indication I had that I was no longer supported by my own federation was a telexed story from a former *Motor Cycle News* reporter. Somewhat more gratifying was a telex sent to Cooper by a number of riders, including Roberts and Uncini, criticising the ACU's move. It read, 'Sheene is an excellent representative who enjoys the confidence of all the riders. Grant chosen to represent not the riders but the ACU.' To Mick Grant's credit, he turned down the nomination, saying he was being used as a pawn in a political game.

The ACU next put forward Jock Taylor, a sidecar racer, who met with almost unanimous approval. He had my backing.

Because of the TT, and the amount of time our delegates spend at the annual FIM Congress discussing that issue, items vital to the long-term well-being of motorcycle racing in general are never put on the agenda. For instance ways and means of attracting more television coverage which, in turn, would have a double-edged effect, are never discussed. Increased coverage would encourage more people to attend live race meetings — and without the paying spectator, professional sport will cease to exist in the form we know it. It would also act as a spur to pull in more European sponsors, without whom there could be no international sport.

It is true that the amount of TV time given over to bike racing has substantially increased in recent years and perhaps 1982 saw television sports editors to be at their most generous. Yet regular showings of the European Grands Prix, along the lines of Formula One motor racing, would drive home to the unconverted public the fact that bike racing at the top level can be as exciting and spectacular as any speed sport.

In 1982, the FIM spent all its time debating the preservation of the TT — to my mind a completely out-dated type of racing that deserves no international recognition because of the dangerous nature of the circuit — and whether or not Italy should be entitled to stage a third Grand Prix because Argentina could not run theirs. Their principal aim should be to find ways in which the sport of road racing can be improved to ensure it exists past the 1980's. But this never comes up.

I can think of any number of experts capable of doing a better job of controlling motorcycle racing, not only in Britain, but worldwide. As long as our top officials continue to complain about riders wanting to drive smart cars and own big houses, they will never truly understand what our respective roles should be in this game.

Why should we agree with their decisions if we believe them to be wrong and know, as everyone does, that it is we, the riders, who can pay the ultimate price?

When I was riders' representative to the FIM, I insisted the Finnish Grand Prix at Imatra should be taken off the international calendar unless the dangerous, tree-lined track which crosses a railway line, could be replaced by a decent circuit. It was OK to race on 30 years ago when the bikes could only do 80 mph but these days a 500cc machine is touching 180 mph. It was a sad reflection on the way our sport is run that it took the death of a top-name former world sidecar champion, Jock Taylor, then acting as riders' representative, before the FIM finally took action.

Imatra lost its 500cc classic in 1982, which meant one less risk to our well-being, one less circuit on which we hated to ride but were coerced by the essential need to collect world championship points wherever GPs took place.

The Czech circuit at Brno and the Nurburgring in West Germany were two more tracks I wanted excluded from the list of Grand Prix circuits.

A circuit with houses, walls, posts, unprotected Armco fencing and severe drops, as at Brno, is no track for a modern 500cc machine. The Nurburgring was impossible to make safe. Over the fourteen-mile round trip, if you missed hitting Armco, the pine trees would catch you, and if someone crashed on the far side of the circuit, the time taken to locate an ambulance or helicopter could easily prove fatal. It was also unfair to the people starting out in the world championship because they needed at least two visits to learn which way the circuit went. The Nurburgring must rank as the circuit I hated most of all.

Because I want to eliminate natural road circuits such as those three, I might stand accused of wanting to rob all tracks of any kind of interesting feature. Let me say there is nothing more featureless than a corpse lying on a mortuary slab. The old type of road circuit has no place in today's racing where, because of the speeds involved, the chances of something untoward happening increases all the time. We have to cut down on those risks, not wait until we have a long list of dead or dying on the official report sheet.

When I clinched my first world title in Sweden in 1976, I had no need to ride in the final three rounds which happened to be on the three circuits in question. Because of the FIM's peculiar points scoring system whereby a rider's best three scores from the first three rounds were added to his best three scores from the remaining five rounds, I know no-one could catch me whatever happened. I had originally stated that I had no intention of riding at those three places because of the danger. So I went straight home. The following year, I made sure of the championship in Finland by coming sixth and so even though the scoring system had changed to make points from all eleven rounds count, I was in a position to politely turn down the Czech invitation.

If there were problem circuits still on the list of GP fixtures, the only fair method of scoring would be one in which the best ten out of twelve rides counted. This would give riders the opportunity to pick and choose the circuits they prefer to compete on. Back in 1975 the best six results from the ten rounds counted in the final analysis, which gave grateful members of the Continental circus the option of avoiding the TT if they so desired. Almost all the name riders at 500cc level felt as I did. One visit there was enough to convince me I could never enjoy racing over the mountain circuit. I've nothing against the island itself. I went there as a boy to watch the TT and my hero Phil Read as much as I could; and good luck to those who take part in the races. Like my friend Bernard Murray to whom I lent a bike, they obviously derive a lot of pleasure racing there, but it's just not my cup of tea.

Now if they purpose-built a track just behind Douglas, and it was safe, I'm sure I would be interested in crossing the water. The same applies to new circuits incorporating safety considerations in East Germany, Czechoslovakia and Finland. But as it stands it's my life I'm risking so I'll choose where to race.

If these horror circuits are deemed unsafe for riders like me, how can the FIM justify their use for their 'Second Division' European Championships where the riders, albeit less experienced than GP contestants, operate machines just as fast as ours?

Greater strides forward must be taken in the cause of track safety: more catch fencing rather than straw bales, wider use of impact-absorbant rubber to act as protection on corners. Banks of tyres should be removed immediately; hit them at 60mph and it's like hitting concrete, a guarantee of broken bones.

If I notice inadequacies in track safety wherever I'm contracted to race, I'll scream for action. And usually what suits me in terms of safety standards, suits other competitors. I've always been heavy on the safety factor — that's the only way of ensuring you stay alive. When I think back on the number of fellow riders who have been killed because safety standards are inadequate, I am filled with greater resolve to make the racer's lot a far, far better one.

The abolition of killer circuits, together with a complete springclean of top-level bike racing, was, of course, foremost in the minds of the world's riding elite in '79, when we attempted to lift World Series Racing off the ground. We were fighting a losing battle against a tried and tested system — but our efforts certainly shook up the FIM.

I had long been completely fed up with the Grand Prix system which seemed designed to make the rider's lot as difficult as possible. So World Series had my complete backing. Forty of us put up £1,000 each to fund the effort. The outline proposal involved a meeting of 250cc and 500cc classes, with two races in each category. No longer cluttered by the mass of different classes of racing, the simplified programme featuring the best riders in the world could then be sold off to television networks everywhere. It promised to be a real humdinger of a show. This should have led to worldwide sponsorship and put bikes on the same footing as Formula One racing. That was the intention.

We agreed in principle to cut out a number of circuits where none of our members would ride — Imatra in Finland, Brno in Czechoslovakia, Germany's Nurburgring and Francorchamps in Belgium if it had not been adequately resurfaced. All were blacked on the grounds of safety. Venezuela and Sweden were also axed because of the high costs of getting there.We agreed to levy a £50,000 fine on any of our member riders who might renege on the deal and ride on those circuits.

We intended to use around eight tracks, mostly in Europe, where the 40 contracted riders would be competing for 200,000 dollars in prize money for each round, an almighty improvement on the FIM deal. There would have been no start money.

Certain sections of the Establishment and the press, particularly the British end, were critical of our motives. They saw this as merely an attempt by some highly-paid riders to take even more money out of the sport. That, of course, was pure nonsense; our aim was to secure better working conditions for everyone. We wanted greater emphasis on safety; a better choice of circuits to race on where there would actually be more than the handful to watch which was so often the case at Anderstorp and Jarama; wider television coverage; and a concerted effort to attract international sponsorship.

With almost overwhelming support from the riders in the early stages and with an alliance with Mark McCormack's International Management Group, whose experience and knowledge of sports sponsorship would provide the link with television, we seemed at last to be in a position to run our own affairs.

I recall Barrie Coleman, a Director of World Series, saying, 'There is nothing very surprising about World Series. What is surprising that it took so long to happen. The professionalism of the riders and the potential of the sport has so far outstripped the management capabilities of its old and feeble democracy.' His words were endorsed by everyone involved in the struggle — and struggle it turned out to be.

The movement began to fall apart from the riders' end. Wil Hartog was the first to pull out, claiming he had a contract from Suzuki which demanded he contest the FIM's version of the world championship. Few people believed that Suzuki had written that clause into his contract and, as a Suzuki man myself at the time, I certainly had not been put under any such pressure.

Hartog made this claim at one of our early meetings in a Brussels hotel to formulate policy and to decide our method of tackling the FIM. Kenny Roberts was most upset. Roberts shouted obscenities at Hartog as he left the room, and there weren't any at that seven-hour meeting who disagreed.

Then riders likely to get a factory contract became hesitant about the whole plan, concerned that the breakaway movement would not get off the ground and worried about losing works support if the Japanese teams chose not to ride World Series.

Then circuit owners, who had originally expressed total support, began to be frightened by the warnings from the FIM. The circuit bosses knew that if the World Series failed the FIM would not sanction their tracks for future Grands Prix, which would have meant losing their biggest pay day of the year.

Everything was happening at a time when I was setting up my own team but I was making arrangements confident I would be racing World Series on decent circuits at meetings run by fair-minded promoters.

I had written into my contract with my sponsors, Akai and Texaco, that I could choose to run in the riders' championship if I wished, and they raised no objections, mainly because they felt my team would get greater exposure in the World Series meetings.

But when Yamaha insisted that Kenny Roberts had to ride in the traditional Grands Prix and after the complete rejection of World Series plans by the President of the FIM, Nicholas Rodil del Valle, when the two sides met in Geneva, collapse was on the way. Rodil was totally inflexible on the subject and he redoubled his efforts to ensure World Series did not succeed by forbidding any motorcycling federation around the globe to deal with us.

Rodil, a Spaniard known for his unbending attitude, seemed resentful of any attempt to pierce the FIM's armour, and the prospect of an alternative competition to their own world championship must have filled his members with horror. It was all too much, far too professional for the FIM.

Vernon Cooper said that Kenny Roberts should have stopped on the dirt tracks of America because of his front-line involvement in getting World Series into operation. Roberts, some thought, was the activist behind the breakaway group, a trouble-maker hell-bent on upsetting the FIM apple-cart. From the time in '79 he handed back the victor's trophy to the organisers at the Spanish Grand Prix, for them to sell or pawn, after they had announced they had insufficient money to pay full start money fees, he seemed determined to engage in a running battle with them.

But Kenny was not alone in waging war. We all felt the same way. Being only in his second European season, however, he was more bugged than most because he was amazed that a world championship could be conducted with its main participants so little involved in its organisation. Those of us who had campaigned in Europe over a longer period began to believe, rightly in the end, that nothing the riders could do would affect the FIM's thinking. I still feel the biggest disappointment in the failure of the World Series launch was the lack of a united stand amongst the riders. If we had stuck together — even if it meant a racing boycott — the manufacturers would have had no-one to ride their machines. As the Japanese producers are heavily dependent on racing to maintain development work on their roadsters, they might have been forced into a position where they had to supply bikes for whatever series the leading riders would contest.

It was a bit of a climb down to be forced to complete in the FIM's world championship after our unsuccessful bid, but in order to earn a living we were left with little choice. Nothing much altered — the prize money had been increased slightly and the circuits we wanted crossed off the calendar no longer enjoyed Grand Prix status. For punishment we were given Zolder as the Belgian GP venue, a diabolical track where it was incredibly difficult to overtake.

Where the machines are concerned, there are certainly more hopes of positive steps forward being taken. Every year the modern racing machine becomes just that little bit easier to ride — handling continues to improve, power bands become wider, braking gets better. There should be little to stop machines becoming even faster although a line has to be drawn when man no longer has the mental or physical capability to control quicker bikes.

The day is not far away, I believe, when racing classes will be restructured so that the blue riband category of the sport will be the 250cc. Advances in technology will allow design engineers to coax as much power out of the 250cc as they can from the 500. Perhaps, by then, a revolutionary type of engine will be in existence. Mechanical development advances at such a pace in the motorcycling world that surprise lurks round every corner.

When the Triumph-3 was clocking 140 mph, people were gasping with astonishment. There would never be anything as quick as that, they declared. The limit had been reached.

Now we are into the age when today's projectile, in the right hands, can top 190 mph.

But the improvement of bikes outstrips the circuits' capacity to cope. The Isle of Man is a case in point. As a circuit, it was fine, donkey's years ago, when everyone was bombing around on Nortons at respectable speeds. Now there are generator engines which produce the equivalent power of a 500 cc Norton.

Bikes just outgrow certain circuits and that's where the traditional tracks where little investment has been made to achieve a secure future, may one day be in jeopardy. Is the track wide enough, smooth enough, interesting enough? Are there adequate run-off areas? What are the hazards, natural and unnatural? Will spectators have the viewing facilities to appreciate the finer points of technological advances? There is much to consider as hundreds of Japanese technicians toil away through the night to continue the march of progress.

Ironically, progress, or the lack of it, saw Britain's own Mallory Park go the wall, one of the really safe circuits. The Leicestershire track held fond memories for me and provided the stage for some pleasing Race of the Year results. I'll always remember going there in 1971 the weekend after I had purchased a 125cc Suzuki twin, and beating the big names of the time, the current world champion Dave Simmonds and Dieter Braun, an established West German GP exponent.

For that Mallory opener, I had only managed five laps of practice because of persistent problems with oiling plugs and there was nowhere near enough time to familiarise myself with its characteristics. The bike certainly lived up to expectations and I took Dave Simmonds on his factory Kawasaki three laps from home to win. That heralded a run of a host of victories in Britain as the Suzuki and I combined to make a fantastic duo.

Then there was the last year of racing at Mallory in '82 in the Transatlantic Trophy series where Marlboro, the sponsors, were offering a cheque for £10,000 to whoever could win all six races in the Easter Competition, a feat never previously accomplished. I came to grief at the Mallory hairpin, to lose the first place that would have given me, as it turned out, the six out of six to take the money. As I came out of the hairpin I was almost set to turn on the power. But the bike refused to turn that final bit and it must have looked like something out of a comedy scene as I just fell against the hairpin wall. The momentary steering lock was due to a steering damper weakness, we later discovered. Roger Marshall took that Mallory race and with it my chance of the big cash prize. But there are no certainties in this game and so I didn't work myself into a lather thinking about what might have been. (It locked again ,in practice, at the following Yugoslavian GP so we threw the damper as far as it would go, much to the puzzlement of one of my mechanics who was convinced the Mallory failure was due to a mistake in my riding.)

To give some indication of the deplorable scale of payments by the FIM for the Grands Prix, the reigning world champion, probably the guy who has pulled in several thousand through the gates, could have gone home in '82 from a round with 400 Swiss Francs — about £110 — exactly the same as privateer Joe Soap in his first world championship meeting. That would be the case if his mount experienced trouble — he'd get barely enough to cover the petrol expenses for his car!

If you are running your own team, as in my case, it was vital to finish no lower than third in a 500cc round just to cover costs. Woe betide you if the gremlins struck. Then you would really feel the pinch.

Since the FIM scrapped the system of paying guaranteed start money dependent on your finishing position in the previous year's standings, the risk of losing is increased. Take a look at the FIM's world championship payments scale for the 500 cc class in 1982. Winner of the race would get 13,000 Swiss Francs (about £3570 at the then conversion rate), second 10,000 SF (£2740), third 7,000 SF (£1920), fourth 5,500 SF (£1500), fifth 4,400 SF (£1200), sixth 3,500 SF (£960) and so on down to 400 SF for coming 26th or below. If a guy failed to get in a quick enough time to qualify for a place on the grid, he would receive the standard 300 SF or £80. If the GP was in Yugoslavia, petrol for the transporter alone would cost £250 to get there and back. It just doesn't make sense.

I could lead a race by a mile and break down on the last lap. If 26 riders come past me as I watched from the sidelines I would get the minimum of £110 — with bills to pay for taking an entourage costing £3,500 to attend the meeting. Or I could break an ankle in practice and come away with just £80.

A few of the GP organisers whom I have known for some years may offer a guaranteed minimum fee for agreeing to take part in pre-race publicity and advertising which would go some way towards defraying expenses. But there has to be an agreed sum, sufficient to cover the outlay. I've no objection to having to earn my money. But why, as a works-supported rider, should I pay to race, which is in fact what is happening? Why should any established runner have to fork out to compete at the world championship meetings?

I would miss the excitement and the glamour of Grand Prix racing, I admit, as I would the chance to bring the world crown back to Britain. But I certainly don't intend paying for that privilege. In fact, I have paid my dues with the Silverstone crash, which meant the 1982 season cost me a lot of money. In '82 I had to pay to race — and I'm not doing it again.

Although the money I obtained to go Grand Prix racing in 1982 was insufficient to cover my costs, I chose to go ahead, banking on it being an investment year. I was confident I would win the world title that would guarantee me factory bikes for '83 and good financial rewards.

But whatever the outcome of my discussions with sponsors and television chiefs, I knew I would be racing a bike somewhere in the year after my Silverstone crash.

Then, of course, there was an exciting prospect of becoming a television presenter. It appeared to be a fresh, exciting challenge that I was red-hot keen to take up. I knew that I could not sit at home waiting and hoping the right sponsorship would come along and so I had to explore every avenue to ensure I had an income. I'm not the sort of person who can sit back and do nothing, even though I have got the financial security I always intended to obtain.

Whenever invitations to appear on television programmes come my way, I'd welcome the opportunity to allow our sport the greatest chance to seize vital exposure. Television is a business I thoroughly enjoy and, with appearances on all kinds of shows, from Swap Shop with Noel Edmonds, to Michael Parkinson, it seems I have made a breakthrough for my sport.

My good run from the mid-seventies has obviously helped to draw new followers into the sport and these have obviously formed opinions on how I race. Hundreds of letters arrive each week, some from five-year-olds just learning to write and others from grandmothers who have seen me on the television. This is an indication of the pulling power of motorcycle racing. It attracts the interest of people of all ages and is followed by a very broad spectrum of the population.

Although I'm the oldest of the crop of factory riders, I feel the advantages in having seniority on my side will be of benefit when battling alongside the best of them over the next few seasons.

The crashes have left no lasting legacy. My movements are fairly much like the next person's although I continually have to avoid crouching down because of the knee injuries.

I was once invited to race a 350 Yamaha at Interlagos in Brazil in an international meeting. The bike, once ridden by former 350 world champion Walter Villa, was completely unfamiliar and, in fact, I had to borrow another 350 for the race because the original performed so badly.

My only memory of the event was being left on the start line by an unco-operative bike and then scaring myself to death in getting up to seventh place.

But my favourite recollection of that South American week was a visit to the gents toilet in the paddock. Upon opening the door, I realised it was a French-style loo where the occupant of the cubicle has to squat down. My limbs were not capable of such a position and so I decided to use the women's toilets where, according to Steph, more conventional sit-down toilets existed. She checked to see there was no-one watching and I rushed in eager to do business.

But I was immediately confronted by a huge mama of a lady toilet attendant who began to rant and rage at me. I had clearly committed a major sin in that part of the world. As I tried to explain the circumstances, my embarrassment increased as the crowd gathered and so I elected to retreat to the pits in the hope practice would be a short-lived enough affair to enable me to get quickly back to my hotel for some blessed relief.

The relief I was seeking after '82 would only come from completing a new season unhindered by mishap but, hopefully, overwhelmed by success. The slice of fortune was owed to me.

Had my enthusiasm for the sport vanished, as it seemed to have done with Graeme Crosby after '82, who went into retirement after only a handful of seasons of Grands Prix, then it would have been extremely hard to re-generate that vital ingredient of all success, dedication.

But not even the misery of the Silverstone smash could detune my devotion to the cause.

My appetite for the sport remains insatiable, continuing evidence that the immense pleasure I obtain from racing a motorcycle has not diminished. When it begins to pall, I will know the time has come to quit.

10
WHY
DO I DO IT?

On one wall of my study, over the leather sofa, hangs a large colour photograph showing a crowd of spectators at a British race meeting. Prominent is a cheery character proudly displaying his tee-shirt which bears the inscription, 'Sheene is a Wanker'.

When I was given the picture, I thought it was hilarious. The guy obviously wore that tee-shirt hoping to upset me. If he knew I had the picture specially framed and had given it pride of place in my home, I'm sure he would be devastated. The greatest satisfaction for someone trying to break you down mentally, comes from letting him know he has pierced your defences. That bloke didn't affect me and nor will anyone else intending to hurt me because of his jealousy.

The back-biting and the sniping that always exists in professional sport began in my case at an early age, although the flak has originated mostly from the traditional element in motorcycling. When my bandwagon of success began to gather momentum in the mid-seventies, some began to use me as a punch bag on which to vent their frustrations. Because in my own way, I was changing the face of motorcylce sport, projecting it into a different galaxy with me as the shining star. The fame, the riches, the glory — they came to me only after a lot of hard work, not to mention considerable pain.

Maybe because I didn't sport a tattoo, wear an ear-ring in my left lobe or drink brown ale, I did not qualify, in some bikers' estimation, as a suitable standard-bearer for the motorcycling fraternity.

But I don't conform to a pattern. I'm Barry Sheene — an individual who likes to do things in his own special way. I live life the way I feel happiest and, if some object, I'm sorry but there is nothing that will change my outlook.

Some complained that I earned too much money from the sport: others took umbrage over the things I have said. That's OK by me. They are perfectly entitled to their opinions. If they honestly feel I'm an asshole, who am I to deny them the freedom to express themselves in any way they want to? I just take comfort in the fact that people who support me form the majority.

At any race meeting I'm quite happy to spend time, in some cases many hours, chatting to racegoers and signing autographs. I find it's no particular hardship. I enjoy being with people. If I did not, I might find fraternisation with the public something of a chore.

Most people I meet with are fine to get on with and to chat to. That says a lot for the sort of person involved in motorcycle sport, which has always been noted for the friendly relationship existing between public and competitors. Of course, there are times when two minutes of boring conversation with a race fan can seem to last a lifetime and you pray for them to move off in a different direction as quickly as possible. But then there are the others. Perhaps a three-year-old will sit on your knee and entrance you with some really off-beat line of questioning, quite possibly not about motorbikes at all. The best fans to meet are those who are natural enough to chat about day-to-day aspects of life, not the heavy enthusiasts who want to get me deeply involved in the finer technicalities of tuning a two-stroke racing engine. As I have said before, there are far more interesting things in life than bikes and I have never wanted my whole life to revolve around two wheels.

These days you have to be more than just a motorcycle racer to make a decent living from the sport. Who does bike racing actually appeal to? Only to the enthusiast. Some riders make no attempt to try to aim at the unconverted. Put a microphone in front of some of the top guys and all you will hear is some dull comment on how trouble-free the ride was. Ask them to talk about anything other than motorcycle racing and it will be a disaster, the end of the conversation.

Some, I have found, are difficult, even embarrassing, to talk to, even in a relaxed atmosphere, because they find it impossible to talk about anything but racing. That doesn't suit me.

To be honest, nowadays I rarely venture out on the highway on two wheels although when I lived in Putney I used to ride only my Suzuki GT750 because it was by far the easiest way to get around London.

When I say I don't ride on the road, people ask me how I can continue to be so keen on racing. The honest answer is that my enthusiasm remains sky-high season after season actually because I just don't eat, sleep and drink motorbikes. I ride them at weekends, albeit at fast speeds on the track, for enjoyment, and a fair bit of the rest of the week is tied up organising the racing team. One of my closest friends, Steve Parrish, happens to be a racer. Others amongst my circle of acquaintances are unconnected with bike racing. In fact, even if Steve was not into racing, I'd still be a mate because we share the same outlook on life. We're out of the same mould.

But I love to race. If anyone else in life comes close to obtaining a similar joy from their vocation, then it must be airline pilots and flight-deck staff. Whenever I fly anywhere, I normally get permission to go forward to the flight deck to observe proceedings, and I've noticed that even though some captains have been doing that demanding job for thirty years, they exude an aura of contentment that can only come from loving what they are paid to do.

Maybe I am the East End barrow-boy who has made good. Perhaps I have earned more than enough, but I've put everything into what was once just a recreation for me. I've hurdled every kind of obstacle put in my path and can say, without exaggeration, that the delight I get from riding a racing machine has never dwindled. In spite of the bleak and agonising periods I have experienced, there is nothing I'd like more than to start my career all over again.

Being obsessed with motorbikes doesn't enter into it. If I was in a field full of different motorcycles around an old Dakota, I'd much rather examine the plane. But riding the bikes in competition always gives me a real buzz.

There's nothing brave about being a motorcycle racer. Assuming you know what you and the machine are capable of and make sure you stick within those limits, it's like any other job. Perhaps I find it more enjoyable than most other forms of work because it's the complete package I've liked — not just the actual competition out on the track but all the other aspects: of planning; bike preparation; finding sponsorship; and so on; that should add up to a successful unit.

Commentators and some national pressmen often wax lyrical over the fact that an inch of tyre rubber on the road is all that keeps a death-defying rider from toppling off at 160 mph, but I don't believe that courage enters into it. People may accuse me of being blase about the qualities of a good motorcycle racer, having been involved in the game for so long, but I have never thought there was anything special about being capable of racing a motorbike. I suppose I'm fortunate in that I don't have to take a deep breath to compose myself as I lean into a bend; the whole thing comes naturally to me. If I sat down before a race and worried about what I was going to do, I wouldn't bother putting my leathers on. I cannot remember the last time I was nervous.

When I go to bed the night before a big meeting, often with half a bottle of wine inside me, my thoughts are miles away from racing. There are far better things to concentrate on. It is not until I get up in the morning that I start to allow the race to occupy my mind.

I learnt the trade as I went along, but even in my first outing at Brands Hatch back in the late sixties, I never thought that racing a bike demanded outstanding talent or any particular bravery. It was never a case of 'Look at me, I'm a big brave motorcycle racer.' What creases me up is the attitude of some riders who seem to want to bury their head in their hands before a race as if to say, 'Don't talk to me, I'm racing in a minute. This could be the last race of my life.' That's a load of baloney. Whilst some might imagine that guys who race fast and well for a living are from a different world equipped with skills available only to a privileged few, I firmly believe that there is nothing out of the ordinary about those competing at my level. You get on the bike, you wind it up and you make sure you steer it in the right direction round the track and round others who aren't doing those simple basics as you pass them. That's all there is to it. Just because I can race a bike, why should I be regarded as something special? I feel prouder of being able to fly a helicopter than I do about riding a racer.

I suppose results prove that I possess something that puts me slightly above many others but I can't say I have given much thought to self-assessment. I have a job to do, I endeavour to do it to the best of my abilities, hoping everything turns out well. Isn't that the purpose of working at any job?

I began racing to have something else to do at weekends than drive a lorry around. It was just luck that I immediately found satisfaction and was fortunate enough to be able to earn a living from it.

I finally gave up other work to go full-time racing because it was getting in the way of my great love for the sport. So any progression of my career was natural rather than being induced. If I was a teenager again, I know that there is nothing I have done I wouldn't do again.

I was asked once what would I have liked to know at eighteen that I know now. I struggled long and hard to think of anything other than wishing I had had a better understanding of people and how their minds work; which ones to trust and which ones to avoid. But everything considered, if I could live it again my life would be re-run in precisely the same pattern. I have no misgivings at all about what I have done in my life. Could everyone say that with as much conviction?

So what about the bleak moments, such as the crashes? Well, they are just lessons in life, the low points that everyone has to endure. Ignore any suggestion that the high number of crashes I have had may have made me immune to the awareness of the dangers of bike racing. I appreciate the danger factors involved, inherent as they are in any sport concerned with fast movement. But I have the same attitude to racing as I did when I first started. I know I could get killed on a bike but I can control fate, given reasonable cooperation from the mechanical well-being of the machine. As long as I continue to enjoy racing a bike, I'll do it and disregard the dire consequences that can befall the unlucky and the unprepared.

Fortune has been on my side to some degree because I've never sustained a bad blow to the head, which has to be the worst enemy of any rider. The thought of being brain-damaged and paralysed from a bad fall scares me out of my wits if I stop to consider it for too long. I'm fully aware I'm involved in a high-risk profession and accidents can happen but, if I wasn't man enough to face up to hazards, I'd get out of the sport.

I frequently get asked why I come back for more punishment immediately after getting over the latest round of injuries. Racing's not an addiction; it is something that continues to give me great pleasure. There are equally hazardous things in life. Smoking can be very harmful, driving in fog, even flying. Look at Graham Hill, killed in a light-aircraft crash after years of risking everything in the seat of a Formula One car. When someone decides your number is up, it's up. So why worry?

Bikes have brought me a marvellous lifestyle. Many people suspected I gathered my first million pounds worth of assets in '76, my first world championship winning year. I wouldn't disagree. But even if I did become motorcycle racing's first millionaire, I don't think those who have seen what I've done over the years would deny that I'm entitled.

There is no doubt that I've earned from racing more than anyone else in history. But it's been a difficult job that could easily have left me redundant, if not dead, at some stage. The rewards can be high, but so can the perils. It's work I love doing and I reckon my results show I'm reasonably proficient at the job. So I get paid well as I knew I would a number of years ago when I first established myself.

My projected plan provided for high earnings, once I had made my name both in Britain and abroad.

Since '74, each season has yielded a better and better return, reaching a peak in 1981 when my earnings must have put me at the top of the earnings ladder in any British sport:

a great year and I just hope I can have a few more like that one. There are other ways of supplementing my income. I could make money during the winter by opening a supermarket or a new store every day. But that just wouldn't be my scene — too much like prostitution of the art.

When it comes to discussions about money with race promoters at major meetings, I never query other riders' terms. You hear a lot of talk about what some riders are or aren't getting in start money for internationals, and the figures bandied about in the press can often be a million miles away from reality. As for me, it doesn't concern me how much others make out of racing. I'm satisfied with what I earn. Having assessed my value to each individual meeting, I lay my cards straight on the table. There is no reason to quibble about my asking price, as I always settle for a reasonable sum — reasonable to everyone involved.

If I'm requesting £10 to race at a meeting and I hear of a rival being paid £100, that's his privilege. I'll only request what I think I'm worth, what will satisfy me, and allow me to race and entertain the crowd. Why should I ask for astronomical sums when I can see that a promoter has not the available cash? I apply the same approach to all my financial dealings. Then, when you put your signature on that contract, you have an obligation to put on the best display you and the bike are capable of. That way you are sure of being invited back. I'm proud to say I've never done a start-money special in my career — and don't intend to. Even if the money is already in your wallet you race as hard as the bike will go.

As far as non-championship races are concerned, I choose to go where I want to ride and if I cannot complete what should be a realistic agreement with a promoter, I won't race that weekend. But, as enthusiasts know, the Grand Prix scene is a completely different kettle of fish. From a monetary standpoint, the world championship is financial bad news for every sort of competitor. The Grands Prix cost me money every time I take part, so it's easy to guess what they do to the privateer with barely any sponsorship, who finds it a struggle even to pay for the fuel to get from one GP circuit to another.

The only reason for contesting the world championship is for investment purposes: do well in the GPs and that provides a means of securing better payment scales in international meetings where the real rewards lie. Of course, high world championship placings bring wider recognition, which in turn attracts advertising and sponsorship contracts. It is regrettable from the point of view of earning a decent living, but you are forced to take part in the world championships to make progress in motorcycle racing, if only because the competition has to be regarded as a platform from which to display your ability to everyone who matters. Fail to contest the classics and so demonstrate your true worth and you're struggling to survive.

There are riches to be obtained by a few but the amount that has to be gambled by the less fortunate, non-contracted lads with no option but to take part in the high-stakes game, can be outrageously large. To have a hope of getting any remuneration out of the sport from the non-championship meetings, you have to enter the world championships where you'll make no money. It's stupid, it's daft, it's absolutely ridiculous. But the Grand Prix system has remained unchanged for a long time in spite of unsuccessful attempts to revolutionise it and I dare say it will continue to run in the same way until kingdom come.

Personally, I've lost a lot of money in Grand Prix racing. It can cost a fortune to attend some of the distant rounds, though the prize money has been increased in recent years. But look what happened when I won the Swedish Grand Prix in 1981. I did my calculations and worked out I made a £600 loss on the whole trip and that's typical of most GPs.

But in spite of the money hassles, I enjoy competing in world championship races. I could ride only in internationals and make a handsome living, but I would miss the annual challenge of the GPs — and when every new season comes round I still believe I'm capable of winning the series.

Yamaha supplied my machines in '81 on the understanding that I took part in Grands Prix. But although they were keen, quite obviously, for me to compete in the televised UK meetings as well, they gave me a free hand otherwise.

The meetings I now appear at each year number about 25 and I think that's sufficient, given the amount of work that has to be done on the machines in preparation for the weekend ahead — riding the bike is the easy part of the job. But I maintain I work harder than most other professional Grand Prix entrants. I'm instrumental in getting the machine set up properly, I give all the instructions in my capacity as team manager and I attempt to negotiate all the contracts necessary to fund the racing effort.

Helping out with the constant search for sponsors are my agents CSS, Britain's largest independent sports promotion consultancy and Julian Seddon, a photographer's agent who knows a lot of people in the advertising world. I think I can claim to be the first rider to compete as a limited company: Barry Sheene Racing Ltd., into which all start money and prize money goes. Acting on expert advice, I formed the company back in 1973 to simplify income tax matters. What it means is that the company foots the bill for parts and bits and pieces while paying me a salary.

Not so long ago, I was invited onto the board of Spectra, makers of car- and motorcycle-care products, as technical director. We use the products when racing so I can make some positive suggestions as to where improvements can be made.

As a bachelor, I started off with a one-bedroomed flat in Holborn and then bought a country mansion in the Fens near Wisbech which was the right distance away from the hustle and bustle of London. I was having a whale of a time with women in the early seventies and needed the chance to go somewhere quiet to calm down. Then I met Steph, and needed somewhere bigger. Because of the need to attend regular meetings with advertising agencies and sponsors in London, it had to be in London, so I obtained a terraced house in Putney. In the twelve months I lived in Putney, I only managed to visit my Wisbech home three times. I missed the country, and since my racing future now looked secure, I sold both properties and went house-hunting.

The house-hunting expeditions took some time and at first I found nothing that met my requirements: it had to be large enough to accommodate my parents in privacy (we are a close-knit family); have workshop facilities and extensive outbuildings for my racing-team work; and be near an airport to enable me to get abroad without difficulty. Easy access to Dover for crossing to the Continent was also an advantage.

Then I found Charlwood, my Elizabethan manor house on the Surrey/Sussex border. I fell in love with it the moment I went up the gravel drive. When I went over the 11th-century, 33-roomed manor and the 22 acres that went with it, I just knew it was tailor-made for me. A fair amount of renovation work needed to be done, but with all its oak beams and inglenook fireplaces, it was a place that I felt I could call home, somewhere I could envisage spending the rest of my days. Noel Coward's actress friend Gladys Cooper was the previous owner, and every piece of building work she had commissioned was designed to enhance its true character. The land that went with it offered plenty of space to breathe, room to land the helicopter, run my Alsatian Nixon and still leave plenty of fields left over for farmers to graze their cattle and locals in the 900-year-old village to keep their ponies. The animals are there to keep the grass short.

My parents have their own self-contained annex in the west wing. We even managed to encourage Steph's parents to move south from Cheshire after their retirement. They now have a place a quarter-mile down the road, and Steph's dad looks after the grounds.

When I bought it, I thought at first about taking out a mortgage, but the interest rates were so frightening I reckoned the best move was to buy it outright though that made a big hole in the savings I had managed to scrape together over the last ten years. Now, if I decide to sell it, I would put it on the market for £400,000. I have always tried to live for today but keep one eye open for tomorrow; so whatever fate decrees, I know I'll always have my house and not owe anybody a single penny.

My racing successes have presented me with opportunities to enjoy to the full a number of my interests in life. One is a partiality for excellent food and drink — particularly Italian food and French wine.

However, I still like the more traditional things, and many of my tastes have remained relatively unchanged since I was a kid. My favourite meal is still the traditional Sunday roast: beef, Yorkshire pudding and the trimmings although I prefer to steer clear of potatoes because I believe their nutritional value to be relatively small. Vegetables and green salads are infinitely better for me, I reckon.

If I have a weakness, it is my passion for good wine. My appreciation of fine wine has grown over the past few years. I'm learning a little more every time I uncork a bottle from the cellar I've tried to build up and I guess Burgundy tops my list of favourites, with Chambertin as the outstanding choice. Ten years ago if someone gave me a five bob bottle of claret, I hadn't a clue as to whether it was old plonk or a splendid vintage. My view then was that wine tasting was a waste of time. Now my taste has matured to such a degree I often buy wine to lay down so that I will be drinking it at its best in a few years' time. But since I enjoy wine with every evening meal, there is little likelihood of purchasing for investment. The turnover is too great!

The other great love in my life is flying the helicopter. Learning to fly it served a dual purpose. I had never previously studied for an exam or obtained any sort of qualification. For me to read a book was unusual and I would usually only consult one to discover how to do something. Now I set myself the target of getting my flying licence in under a month, before going to Venezuela for a water-skiing holiday. As well as purely flying instruction, there was a huge amount of book work: aviation; navigational techniques; meteorology.

I pored over text books and stretched my studies into the early hours of the morning. It was hard work, but the effort paid off, and I passed each exam stage with high marks.

I think the reason I was so determined to get my helicopter pilot's licence so quickly was that I wanted so desperately to fly. My only outside assistance came from a friend who once flew my Piper — he could supply answers to my questions in certain grey areas — and from two excellent flying instructors at Shoreham who put me through the compulsory 35 hours in the air before I could sit the exams.

Now I've got my wings, the feeling I experience every time I'm in flight is so exhilarating. The American three-seater Enstrom 280 Turbo will take me from Gatwick to Manchester, given favourable wind conditions, without needing to refuel. That's about two and a half hours flying time, with a top speed of 117 mph. She drinks about 11 gallons of aviation fuel an hour, but even so it is nowhere near as expensive to fly as many might think. It's only marginally more pricey to run than a Rolls.

Now if I have to make a long journey on business, I leave the car in the garage and take the helicopter. It's quicker, far more relaxing and ends the constant risk of getting booked for speeding. Once I climbed back into the helicopter after the Silverstone crash, I knew I was really on the mend.

So as far as cars go, my main car these days is a Mercedes 500 SEL, which is the German company's top-of-the-range model. We also have a Mazda pick-up and a Suzuki jeep for general running around. I put my Rolls up for sale after my Silverstone crash. It had been sitting in the garage for ages and it seemed pointless just letting it lie there.

Although I'm tremendously patriotic, I have to admit that for me the Mercedes combined the good looks of the Porsche and the grace of the Rolls. I regularly motor 30,000 miles annually, or I did before I brought the helicopter, but the Rolls had only 25,000 miles on the clock after three years. That Shadow 11 was the third Rolls I've had. Even as a boy, I had set my heart on getting a Rolls, although I can't think why I thought it might become a reality, because I was working as a storeman in a car parts warehouse when the dream first overtook me. The first one I bought in the mid-seventies was so trouble-free it was my idea of the perfect car — something you get into, turn the ignition key and set off, with no likelihood of trouble. It carried me 30,000 miles a year, and the second one did 22,000 in the first six months without a single hitch. The Rollers had everything I wanted from a vehicle, including plenty of room inside, bags of boot space to sling the gear, and a useful role as part of the image building.

I eventually got round to having a sports car when I did some testing for television at the Motor Show. I drove a Porsche 928 and commented that it needed more power and better brakes, although it was the most comfortable car I had driven. But Porsche were about to bring out the 928S which had a bigger engine and so I ordered one. It was enjoyable, with a quicker motor, but of course, it had to be sold eventually to finance my racing.

My job has taken me all around the world apart from Australia and New Zealand but, strangely enough, I've never had a burning desire to travel. Most people would be green with envy at my opportunities to see different places, but apart from Venezuela, there's really no place I'm happier to be in than England.

My dress sense isn't particularly sharp and I'll never need a personal tailor. There's not even one suit in my wardrobe. I just wear casual clothing in which I feel comfortable, which means I'm normally in jeans every day of the year. In fact, I'm paid to wear jeans. I have a contract with a jeans company to demonstrate their brand. But that's incidental. If I want to pull on a pair of jeans, no-one is going to stand in my way. What makes me laugh is the attitude of some hotels or restaurants who forbid you to wear jeans. A suit must be worn, they command. But it doesn't matter to them if the jeans and jumper have just been cleaned and pressed and are as fresh as a daisy. A guy will happily be welcomed, wearing a dirty old suit that hasn't been to the cleaners for six months, and a smelly, filthy shirt. To me, those double standards are total bullshit, sheer hypocrisy. You're supposed to be a nice person because you're in a suit. The fact that your underpants haven't been changed for six months is neither here nor there, apparently.

There was an occasion when we intended taking my

mother out to celebrate her birthday, with dinner at a local restaurant not far away from my home. When I reached the door, some flunkey asked if I could go back and change, as jeans were not permitted. Ridiculous. The chap who owned the place wouldn't, if asked, have changed his dress to suit my tastes, so why should I have done the same? And why should someone be put off their dinner because I'm not wearing a tie? I left and will not go back.

I can accept that a banquet may demand a dicky bow and a tuxedo. That's fair enough, and it's why I don't accept invitations to functions like that. If the invitation states 'black tie', this rules me out. It's not a case of my rebelling against society's rules; it's just that I like to do what I want to do. I dress to please myself, not other people. The last time I put on a suit was in 1977, when I had to go to Buckingham Palace to receive the MBE from the Queen. The importance of the occasion gave me no option but to dress up. The gilt-edged invitation card mentioned 'Morning dress or dark suit'. Me in top hat and tails would have been total insanity. Could you imagine it? So I settled for a dark suit and tie, which made me feel slightly strange. As I was allowed to take two guests with me, I chose Mum and Dad because of the enormous backing and support they had given me. Steph said she didn't mind staying at home. I'll come next time, she remarked. Wonder if she was being serious?

Being awarded the MBE came out of the blue. When I heard the good news that my racing achievements and my road safety work had been noticed in high places, I was delighted. Fancy me meeting the Royals.

I did the road safety stuff because I don't like to see motorcycling get a bad name. In any case, if by lending my name to a safety campaign I could save just one life and prevent one family suffering, then it would have been a worthwhile contribution. I don't enjoy ordinary riding because I'm so aware of the dangers that seem to lurk everywhere. I ride assuming that every other road user is a complete idiot and that they are capable of doing something completely outrageous. So as I'm concentrating so much on what is going on around me it feels like any bike journey is taking me hours to complete. It means I'm not getting that relaxed feeling biking would once offer. Even if it's a dead straight road completely devoid of traffic, my eyes are sweeping ahead of me for anything that might suddenly become a hazard.

Once on a clear road, a fox ran out of the hedgerow right across my path and I didn't even have time to touch the brakes. Luckily I just glanced it and as I was only doing around 50mph, I got away unscathed, as did the fox.

Meeting the Queen was quite an illuminating experience. We shook hands and she asked me if I thought I could win the world championship again the following year. I said I hoped I could. 'You be very careful then,' she said. I replied, 'Well it's not so dangerous as riding horses.' The Queen just laughed. She was very charming and far prettier than her photographs, which don't do her justice.

Though the MBE made me feel very proud, I never carry the letters after my name and I seldom think about it. I can't say it affected my life much or the way people treated me. The medal itself is nothing to write home about but the signed scroll is neat, with Elizabeth R's signature at the bottom.

I seldom watch much television apart from the news but I get a kick out of appearing on it, just like anyone else. On the Michael Parkinson show I have guested with Sir Ralph Richardson, Michael York, Willie Carson and Dudley Moore — all fascinating people whom I enjoyed chatting to after the show. Then there was the notorious Russell Harty show where I invited him to feel the plating in my broken left leg after the Daytona crash. He invited me back on his programme last winter. I wondered if he had a fetish about broken legs. He only seems to want me when I've got a smashed limb.

The greatest shock, though, has to be my appearance on 'This is Your Life'. Still jet-lagged after getting back from Japan, I had Maurice Knight, the racing chief from Heron Suzuki, on the phone to me pleading with me to go to the Racing and Sporting Show in London to do a televised interview for a 'Drive-in' programme. I explained that all I wanted to do was to sleep.

Then Gerald Ronson, boss of the Heron Corporation, contacted me. 'Do it as a personal favour for me!' he said. I should have realised that for him to concern himself with what looked like being just another interview meant something was up. What should have blown the whistle was the sight of Stephanie wearing a dress. Like me, she's hardly ever out of jeans.

I have always doubted that the subject doesn't know beforehand what is about to happen. But I was completely taken by surprise when Eammon Andrews burst through the film screen to confront me with his book. What a night that was!

The television advertisement campaigns I have featured in have also helped to spread the Sheene gospel; like the Christmas television commercials with Henry Cooper for Fabergé, and the Texaco oils advert working alongside Michael 'Frank Spencer' Crawford.

The relationships I have built up with these companies will, I feel, be useful in years to come when I quit racing and have to earn a living in a less dramatic way. Companies of that standing are important. To be associated with them enhances your reputation and lifts you out of the ruck, helping to dispel the generally held public view that racing motorcyclists are dull fellows away from the track, who have to struggle to string three interesting words together. I like to broaden my horizons and let it be known that one or two of us at least can look further than the end of the finishing straight. And I know that when I retire from racing, I will go potty without anything to do.

Motorbike racing, like so many other industries today, is feeling the cold wind of recession and there are no longer the same number of companies about with the resources to back racing teams. It's not worth the price of a phone call contacting solely British concerns to seek support, because they are going through such a bad economic patch. The only sponsors at the moment with the financial clout to provide adequate sponsorship are multi-national outfits or British set-ups exporting extensively throughout Europe. Even this latter category seems to be dwindling all the time. But Britain's not alone, of course, in going through a recession. Riders from other countries are also struggling to attract the money their racing effort demands.

The downward trend in attendances is apparent in every spectator sport. After all, the first things to go in a recession are unnecessary items. It's not vital for people to watch sport; it is necessary to eat. So I don't think sponsors are shying away because bike racing has something dramatically wrong with it which is turning away spectators. Abroad, crowds are still huge at most Grands Prix.

Constant travel enables me to see problems worldwide, and not just financial ones. Reading a local newspaper in a Buenos Aires restaurant before the Argentinian Grand Prix in the spring of '82, I realised that trouble over the Falklands was imminent. Perhaps I should have phoned the Defence Minister! After the race meeting, an old lady came up to me and insisted in Spanish, 'We want the Malvinas'. I shrugged my shoulders to suggest I knew nothing about the situation. Then, only a few days after getting home, the whole thing blew up. I'm glad we returned when we did.

If there is ever going to be another Argentinian world championship round, and the country's economics look certain to rule it out, I'll have to go there to race, whether I like it or not, if I have designs on the world championship. If I have to go to earn points, then I shall be there with a completely closed mind on what has gone on before. I don't select where the rounds are to take place and I'm left with little choice, if I want to regain the title, but to go where the action is.

The same goes for that other controversial country, South Africa. I won't be going there on a joy-ride to make money. My visit will be purely and simply to try to collect the valuable points as part and parcel of my world championship bid. Competing in a South African GP, I know, causes me to run the risk of going on the sporting black list which means I will not be allowed to go to Communist countries. But that's OK, because I hate Communist countries and all their political doctrine stands for.

My instincts have always made me steer clear of political issues. It's just not worth getting involved because, whatever your views, you're sure to upset somebody. I'm one of those who feel unhappy about the high unemployment figures and I don't condone everything they've done, but I vote Conservative because they have tried to and succeeded in bringing down the inflation rate. Listen to the Labour Party delegates wrangling amongst themselves at their annual conference. How can they inspire confidence in their ability to govern the country? Sure, they could reduce the number out of work but at the cost of having inflation soar to 20 per cent, I'm convinced.

But whatever the tax situation in this country, I would never contemplate becoming a tax exile as have numerous sportsmen before me. When I was seventeen, working as a motorcycle messenger boy and earning only enough to get by, I was happy. I'm no happier now, though I'm banking far more. So why should I allow money to be my God and want to worship it somewhere outside Britain?

This is the country in which I was born and bred and the one I love. I could have been a whole lot richer had I become a tax exile but I wouldn't have been happy living anywhere else but here in Britain.

My whole life does not revolve around money, anyway; what is important is being contented and getting out of life what you want from it. I started racing with very little money and, had I failed to make anything out of it, I would possibly still be popping down to Brands Hatch most weekends. The moment I stop deriving enjoyment from the sport I'll pack up. But while it's my job, my livelihood on which I depend to live and to eat, I expect to get paid for the work I do.

The icing on my personal cake is my girl friend Stephanie. We've been happily together, more or less as man and wife, since '76, but that doesn't mean she shackles me to the home. I'm my own man and do the things I want to do. It so happens that those things meet with her full approval. The boogeying days when I was out at discos most nights have long gone. Now, after dinner, I may pop down to the local hotel to have a couple of brandies, and read the *Financial Times* and admire the scenery, which is usually improved by the comings and goings of pretty air hostesses from Gatwick. But then it's straight home and off to bed.

Steph, or Doreen as I sometimes call her, knows me as well as anybody now and she realises there is little point in placing restrictions on me. It wouldn't do much good. But I never stray far from home when I'm not racing and, more often than not, she is by my side.

So many people have said the accident must have improved our relationship, brought us closer together in a time of crisis. In reality, it did nothing for the relationship because there was no room for improvement. It was ideal before and still is. We seem to be perfectly suited. Maybe it helps that we were both born under the sign of Virgo.

Steph works non-stop about the house doing all those housewife's chores that men come to expect as the norm. I only have to put a tee-shirt in for washing one day and it's cleaned, ironed and back on the shelf by noon the next day.

Her son by her marriage, Roman, comes over to stay with us during the summer holidays. He lives in Beverly Hills with his dad, Clive, a professional fashion photographer. It is better all round for him to live with his father, because Steph and I travel about Europe for so much of the year.

Steph's ex-husband and I get on well together. Under the circumstances he could have been difficult about the whole affair but he accepted and understood the situation. There was never any animosity.

I am frequently asked when I will marry Stephanie and I normally reply that I'll get hitched when we feel we are ready to have children. As it stands, our domestic set-up is good fun and enjoyable and a piece of paper saying we are legally wed wouldn't make the slightest difference to our happiness. We never even talk about marriage.

One day we may want a family. But now is not the time. Motorcycle racing and children don't mix. Not because of the risk, but because I feel kids deserve to have a settled upbringing in one stable place with the prospect of a good education undisrupted by spells away from school with their parents. Travel could ruin the whole thing. The mother would have to stay home to look after the family and that would be the quickest way to spoil a good relationship.

11
BACK AGAIN...

Christmas Day of 1982 was just 72 hours away. The sun was already high in the West African sky as I settled by the pool-side at my luxury Gambian hotel.

The tropical warmth of this final stage of my winter holiday was beginning to relax me once more, and as the busy waiter scurried away with an order for a king-size orange juice, I reflected on the amazing five months just passed. Life, I thought, had become decidedly better since the dark days after the Silverstone crash.

From a physical point of view, my body was in the kind of shape few would have thought remotely possible after the smash-up. I could walk reasonable distances without discomfort and without the aid of sticks. I could crouch down, and could complete a full range of exercises. Swimming was another activity I could undertake, confident that my legs — still pinned and plated — would benefit from sustained energetic activity.

In fact, remedial exercises were no longer vitally necessary. I was nearly back to normal! Now I had to concentrate on my programme of fitness conditioning to get into peak condition for the start of a new racing season.

But I felt good, helped by the satisfaction that the results of a recent brain-scan revealed that the grey matter had not suffered in the pile-up. Some weeks after the accident, I had had bouts of dizziness whenever I put my head back and I wondered, with some anxiety, if my skull had been damaged when I went down the Silverstone track. The diagnosis was reassuring. I had simply contracted an ear infection which had the effect of temporarily upsetting my balance. Antibiotics soon cleared that up and my whole physical condition and the pace of my recovery left me in a really contented frame of mind.

Adding to my happiness was the prospect of working for a new Japanese manufacturer, an association which promised to last until past my retirement from the sport of motorcycle racing. My return to Suzuki was almost like a reunion with old friends after a three-year separation. I had never lost contact with those who ran the British end of the Suzuki operation and I had always had a sneaking admiration for the professional way they conducted their affairs.

In all honesty, though, I cannot recall one occasion when I regretted leaving Suzuki to race Yamahas, because I believed I had made the right decision at the right time.

Even when Suzuki regained the world championship from Yamaha in '81, a period in which they established dominance over Yamaha, I never wished I had stayed put.

The move at the end of '79 was made with considerable forethought, and I had proved it was not a disastrous choice: by the end of the third season with Yamaha I had put myself into a position where I had a chance of landing the prized world crown.

The three years spent in association with Yamaha — one as a privateer and two as a factory-backed rider — were, in the main, happy ones. I found a fair amount of satisfaction in riding their machines, which had helped me collect a wide selection of honours.

But there were numerous aggravations I could have done without. The chief complaint, of course, was that I was continually regarded as Yamaha's 'second son' when it came to getting the best bikes. Kenny Roberts ruled, as far as the hottest bikes were concerned, and it was galling to have to make do with second best.

When I signed a contract for the 1981 season to ride official works bikes for Yamaha I was given a pledge that I would be allocated similar bikes to those given to Roberts. That promise came from the President of Yamaha. But, as I have explained in other chapters, that guarantee was never fulfilled. I would always be one step behind Kenny, the guy Yamaha looked upon as *the* development rider.

It became apparent that the factory's intention was to allow me to have whatever Roberts was presented with — but after a delay of several months.

Being the newcomer in the team, I was prepared to play second fiddle to Kenny during my first year as a contracted rider. There was no reason to believe the situation would not improve both from the point of view of the bikes and of the money they were paying me, the following year. How wrong I was!

For the ill-fated '82 season, I had literally to beg for machines from Yamaha Japan. In their infinite wisdom, the Yamaha supremos felt it would be in everyone's interests for me to compete in Giacomo Agostini's Marlboro cigarette-backed team, which was to be based in Italy, almost certainly at Bergamo, the home of the former MV Agusta world champion.

Although I was never given a complete explanation for their eagerness to send factory Yamahas to Agostini, I figured they wanted to reduce the number of works bikes they had to produce for European riders and I guess Ago had put forward a reasonable presentation to the top brass in Japan. I was given to understand that he had been promised factory bikes and so the provision of a further two for my team clearly meant more work for Yamaha.

But being in an Italian-based outfit wasn't for me. Neither my mechanics nor myself wanted to uproot ourselves from homes close to the team's workshops. The domestic upheaval would have been pointless and unwelcome. Besides, I was more than happy running my own team and obviously did not relish the prospect of being under the orders of a team manager with whom I had previously had little contact.

With full backing from Mitsui, the British Yamaha importers, and from Yamaha's European headquarters in Amsterdam, I argued long and hard with the head office in Japan. I thought that Agostini's team would be less well organised than my own; I would be unsettled operating out of a foreign country; and on the top of that, Ago wanted fifty per cent of all my start money and would require me to support the sponsors he had found to pay for the team's race programme. However much money came from Marlboro, I thought there would not be a vast amount to distribute through the team.

I became very convinced that the venture would be a failure after a meeting with Ago and John Hogan, Marlboro's sponsorship administrator in Europe, in a hotel in Lausanne in Switzerland. The initial contract money was attractive enough, and the deal would possibly have left me better off than if I had wanted to go it alone with my own machines. But happiness was of over-riding importance, not only for me but for my mechanics, who, I knew, would have felt unhappy about working in Italy. As it turned out, conditions and working atmosphere for those in Ago's set-up were far from ideal in the 1982 season.

The pressure was really on me to sign up for Ago's team even though I was supposed to be riding for Mitsui. However, the Japanese appeared to relent once Mitsui had pointed out, quite rightly as my paymasters, that my outings on British tracks in front of their potential buyers would be severely limited if I was connected with an Italian organisation that could dictate where I rode.

I went to Yamaha almost on bended knees to have my own factory machines and it was representations from Steve Hackett of Mitsui and Paul Butler in Amsterdam that made them have a change of heart. At long last, I was to be given works tackle, albeit somewhat outdated tackle compared to that presented to Roberts. But at least I did not have to be part of the Italian organisation, which I knew would have been disastrous for me.

As Ago was still looking round for a number one rider after I had turned him down, I suggested to Graeme Crosby, the easy-going New Zealander, that it could be worth his contacting Italy with a view to filling that empty saddle. Graeme, who, contrary to popular belief, didn't breathe fire every time we met after our Silverstone incident back in '81, was on the verge of signing to race four-stroke Hondas in American Superbike meetings. That was something I'm sure he didn't particularly want so he jumped at the chance to contest the Grands Prix on a factory bike. I thought I had done him a good turn, but when he flew home at the end of his first season with Ago, apparently completely detuned by the whole scene and threatening to quit the sport for good, it seemed he had had the misfortune to suffer the very problems I had anticipated would surround me, had I joined the Italian team.

Happy to have factory Yamahas in my own stable while grudgingly accepting a nil increase in personal terms for the '82 season, I dismissed doubts about Yamaha's loyalty towards me, and began to think confidently of winning the world title for a third time.

My complaints about getting inferior bikes to Roberts seemed to fall on deaf ears. Their excuse that Kenny was the development rider and that I would be handed the machine in an ideal state once the teething troubles had been eliminated cut no ice with me.

In my opinion, Kenny would have difficulty developing a cold, let alone a motorbike. As I have said before, he is hopeless as a test rider. His bikes start by not handling and end up still not handling. It was the same with tyres when he was three years with Goodyear. In all that time, he was unable to come up with information that would help the technicians to make a better tyre.

I would always be waiting until Kenny had developed the latest model. That arrangement was no use to me. I needed to be on a par with everyone else and I began to see that would never be the case as long as Kenny remained top dog with Yamaha. I could tolerate that situation for only so long.

What encouraged me to ignore Yamaha's unsympathetic attitude was my personal belief that I would win the world championship — in spite of the handicap of having lesser machinery — and would place myself in an excellent bargaining position. Once the opening round in Argentina was under way, I knew I would have a fighting chance of finishing top and would have wagered any kind of money against being out of the first three.

I made a special point, during my stay with Yamaha, not to slag off or denounce the shortcomings of the empire, unlike others in Yamaha's employ who could get away with criticising the company's products. 'They don't even make good road bikes,' was one comment from someone who should have known better than to sound off in the press about those who call the tune.

Though I attempted to exercise diplomacy and tact whenever I dealt with the Japanese, one enemy I seemed to make in the Yamaha camp was the team manager. For reasons unknown, he could never seem to take to me. As his position required a fair amount of liaison with me, this made life somewhat awkward for the pair of us. While I was able to get on with all other Yamaha officials, especially those in the export department, the team manager seemed to have difficulty in accepting that I was in the Yamaha team alongside Roberts.

His hang-up over me meant that Roberts' team and mine operated as separate units. We seldom had adjoining pits at race meetings and there was little exchange of ideas over the performances of our respective machines. Perhaps the team manager might have brought us closer together had he not been so ambivalent towards me.

When I heard that Roberts had taken delivery of his new 500-4 for the first time in the Austrian GP at the Salzburgring in '82, I sauntered over the paddock to his awning to check it out. I wanted to see what master-stroke the Yamaha development experts had pulled this time. As I drew back the curtain, my way was blocked by the team manager — *my* team manager.

'I'm with Yamaha too. I'm supposed to be a factory rider,' I pointed out to him.

'Sorry, can no let you see,' he replied.

Completely bemused by his strange attitude, I made no further attempt to get a close-up of Kenny's new model and wandered off. Some time later, after I had casually mentioned that I had been denied access to the bike to Paul Butler, the helpful Yamaha public relations chief for Yamaha's European interest, the team manager specifically came over to my motorhome to invite me to examine the V-4. I felt like suggesting what he could do with the V-4 but, knowing that others more on my side must have given the team manager certain advice, I accepted the man's kind offer.

That was a typical example of Yamaha's inconsistent approach. It was often difficult to understand or to appreciate certain decisions they would reach. The one hardest to fathom was their blind faith in Roberts, a faith that saw Kenny as being the only winner for Yamaha. Yes, he was a god to them. Yet the object of the exercise was, surely, to have a rider win the big events on a Yamaha, irrespective of who that bloke was.

When I won my last GP for Yamaha at Anderstorp in Sweden, they seemed almost disappointed that I had actually triumphed for the factory. It began to seem as if they were doing everything in their power to prevent me from winning — the delay in supplying me with the latest bikes being a prime example. Highly delighted at crossing the line first, I expected the Yamaha mechanical entourage to come across to offer some kind of congratulation. But apart from Kel Carruthers, Kenny's chief mechanic, no-one else from Yamaha came to see me. Not a word from them. That struck me as being rather strange and was possibly further evidence that I was no longer wanted within their ranks.

I still believe that Roberts was unperturbed about having me as his partner in the works team for two years. Being rather different characters and having very little in common we tended not to spend too much time in each other's company, but there was no animosity. I could not say, in all honesty, that he was my best friend in racing, but it is fair to say we respected one another's ability on the track, and we would try to help each other when problems arose.

I was aware that he would have preferred to have a Stateside team-mate during the GP campaign, so it came as no shock to learn that Eddie Lawson was being primed for the job of understudying Kenny. What was surprising was that Yamaha intended embarking on what was basically a European-based world championship with two Americans with whom spectators might find difficulty in relating. Few would even have heard of Lawson.

I had long since accepted that the Yamaha race department seemed not to know their left hand from their right, but when they began talking about drafting in Lawson, it made me realise that their thinking would never be consistent. Yamaha's European network pushed my case strongly with headquarters in Japan. They considered the ailing motorcycle market in Europe needed a recognised figure fronting the racing attack to promote sales of their machines. There was even a promise from Sonauto, the French importers of Yamaha, to support me and a full works championship team if works tackle direct from the factory was unavailable to me.

But it appeared that the engineering department at Yamaha, possibly encouraged by an occasional comment from Roberts, were less than keen to have me with them for a third time. The machine I would have needed in '83 would have been a long time coming, I was convinced.

If they had told me that there were likely to be delays in receiving the latest hardware, I would have been completely in the picture. But Yamaha promised me new bikes on certain dates and they did not materialise. I just don't like being messed about.

By the time of the Belgian Grand Prix in '82, the race chief for Yamaha was surprised I was getting the square-four model to go so well. I reckon he had anticipated me finishing well down the field on this, the previous year's model, instead of elevating myself into a position where I could challenge the best the world could offer.

It was then that the first mention during the season of team tactics was made to me. They would very much appreciate it if I could help out Roberts who was doing not quite as well as expected on the new V-4. I quickly pointed out that I would willingly assist Roberts if there were merely a couple of rounds left in the series and he was within striking distance of the championship. But I told them I was fairly sure I could make the championship mine that season and I saw no reason why I should stay behind Roberts. In any case, the instructions at the start of the season had been crystal clear. Both Roberts and I could ride to win every time unless there existed a situation where one could help the other near the end to collar the title. I suppose I didn't endear myself to Yamaha any more for adopting that stance. As it turned out, I came second after taking Roberts, who finished fourth. Had I acted on the team boss's orders, Yamaha's highest placing would have been fourth.

Faced with a bitter struggle to obtain full support from Yamaha, an increasing amount of disharmony amongst the Japanese back-up squad, and a fight to attract adequate financial backing, I should have wavered in my conviction that I could beat all-comers to the world title. But the problems only succeeded in increasing my determination to finish top of the pile.

As the hassle continued and my disillusionment with the Yamaha organisation intensified, a chance meeting in the Assen paddock before the Dutch TT in June of '82 with Denys Rohan, Suzuki GB's motorcycling managing director, opened up a fresh avenue to explore.

The way Yamaha had been treating me left me in no doubt that I could not be sure things would improve with time. Therefore all options had to be kept open, and so when the conversation between Denys and me over a cup of instant coffee in the Suzuki motorhome switched from general pleasantries to future plans, both of us sensed there was room for further discussions. I had had enough of being overlooked by Yamaha and felt that the long friendship I had enjoyed with the Suzuki GB officials might prevent such an occurrence happening again, if I chose to return to the firm that had set my career rolling. I don't crap on people and I don't expect others to crap on me. I felt Suzuki would honour their word once an agreement had been reached.

More in jest than anything else, I commented to Denys, 'You never know — one of these days, I could be back with your lot.' He must have guessed that not everything was sweetness and light in my relationship with Yamaha. I could also tell from his manner that he might welcome me back. Seeds began to be sown.

By the end of autumn my mind was made up. Yamaha were talking loosely about allocating me a pair of V-4's for '83 right from the start, but it was difficult to obtain a precise commitment from them. Their racing plans were somewhat hazy and I figured I would remain in an uncertain position with them. It was not definite that I would be given the latest machines as and when they were put together and I knew I no longer wanted a bellyful of those problems over a further twelve months.

There was no further contact with Suzuki until a few weeks after I had returned home after leaving hospital following my Silverstone accident. Peter Agg and his son Charles, who live just a few miles from my place, dropped in for a social drink and we soon started talking about the possibilities of my riding again for Suzuki. I felt they wanted me and I knew it would be a good move on my part. We came to a gentleman's agreement almost there and then. The rest of the package quickly and easily took shape.

By the time Yamaha were sounding me out, still not completely convinced I would be in the right condition to do an adequate job for them, I had virtually signed on the dotted line for Heron Suzuki GB. They knew I spoke in all honesty when I said I should be fighting fit by the start of the new season; they recognised that my determination to succeed remained sky-high. In turn, I believed Suzuki's word would be their bond when they outlined what they could provide for me.

Suzuki were quite definite about what they would give me. From the beginning of the '83 season, I would have two standard production RG500 racers to help me pace myself after being almost seven months out of the saddle and to act as an indicator to my level of fitness. There would also be some 'trick' parts built into the machines. Denys Rohan gave me the encouraging news that better machines could be placed in my hands at a later date once I was back to my old form.

I was completely confident I would be tuned in both mentally and physically right from the word go, although I recognised that push-starting the bike might present some difficulty, remembering my first race at Le Mans in '76 upon my return after breaking a leg. It had been a struggle getting the Suzuki off the line.

Both sides appreciated that my legs might take some time to return to full strength, so it would have been one hell of a gamble to give me full works machines from the outset. To allow me to have the best machines would have been politically insensitive, after Suzuki had pared the number of works racers for '83 down to two — Franco Uncini and Randy Mamola.

As I was fully informed by Suzuki about the type of machinery I would be supplied with, and agreed to a delay in allocating me the quickest bikes, I was optimistic our partnership would be an amicable one — almost as it had been the first time round.

When I had departed from Suzuki, it wasn't on bad terms. There was no acrimony — and I had already known full well, during that difficult first year on private Yamahas, that I could have gone back to Peter Agg to try to rebuild my career with Suzuki. I believe he would have had me back. We had known each well enough for many years and, no matter what minor disagreements we had had, we always emerged from disputes as friends.

The slight bother we had in '79 about where my machines should be stabled was no longer relevant. I later understood it was the Japanese and not Heron Suzuki GB who demanded the racers be maintained at the official Croydon workshops, which meant a lot of personal travelling time for me. Now Suzuki's race shop lies only a few miles away from my home, so no problem exists.

I know I owe a lot of gratitude to Peter Agg for what he did for me in the past and it was this level of respect which encouraged me to rejoin his team.

It all dates back to the end of the '75 season. My career as a motorcycle racer might well have ground to a halt then, when my employers, Suzuki Japan, decided to curtail their racing programme. The 500cc machine thay had expected would sweep the board the moment it was pieced together was, in their eyes, almost a lost cause, and the capital outlay appeared to be exceeding budget.

Aside from my comments, which were favourable, the Suzuki boffins were receiving bad reports of their Grand Prix bike and it was clear that my lone voice was not going to prevent them from burying the machine up in a corner of their race shop. The news came as a bombshell. One minute I was a full works runner, confident I could capture the world championship, the next I was out of a job.

The words in the official letter from Suzuki informing me of their abandonment of what should have been a successful third year's partnership between the two of us are still imprinted on my memory.

'Dear Barry,

Our decision to withdraw from direct factory support of the world championship is no way to repay you for all your efforts in our long and extensive development programme...'

It was a ridiculous move to pull the Suzuki out of the action when we had come so far. The bike was on the brink of being the winner I had always anticipated it being, although that view was not shared by many others at the time. Among the pessimists must have been the Suzuki factory technicians.

But it was the foresight and enthusiasm of one man who acknowledged the potential of this particular bike. Peter Agg, now chairman of Heron Suzuki GB, importers of the marque to these shores, had relayed to me the bad news of the end of Suzuki Japan's direct involvment in GP racing. Then, in the next breath, he told me his organisation intended to fund the expenses of running a full team to contest the world championship under the British banner.

A man known for his astute business acumen and experienced enough to appreciate what a winning Suzuki ridden by a Briton could do for home sales, he had arranged that his three-man team be supplied with the necessary machinery and parts from Japan. Joining me in the team would be John Williams and John Newbold, two guys who knew their way round the Grand Prix scene. Sadly, both are no longer with us.

When Peter unveiled his plans to me, my relief was pretty obvious. I still had the bike I believed would take me on to greater heights and I would be contesting the world championship in an outfit that was virtually all British. Had Peter not elected to front the GP effort, I am not sure what would have happened. I guess I might have been riding private Yamahas if Peter's approach had not met with success. He had salvaged something out of the factory's disenchantment and, without any doubt, had not Suzuki GB offered to tackle international racing, the record books would have few mentions of Suzuki in the eighties.

Another hurdle to surmount in renewing acquaintance with Suzuki was to ensure that certain technicians at Hamamatsu bore no grudge against me for what I had said publicly in the late seventies. My criticisms — voiced in another chapter — of one or two Suzuki personnel were valid at the time. I still stand by my word. My opinions were honest and even though I am back working for some of the guys who caused me anguish, I see no reason to retract a word.

The situation is the same as that which existed when I went back to Yamaha. In 1972, I was constantly complaining about the engineering of the bikes, but eight years later I had no worries about mixing with many of the same technicians about whose work I had complained. The fact that resentment may have lingered on failed to bother me and, if there is still an anti-Sheene faction amongst the Suzuki ranks in Japan, I'll have to grin and bear it. For my part, it was to be a case of forgiving and forgetting. My fresh alliance with Heron Suzuki GB rekindles memories of the occasion back in '73 when I attempted to obtain a crashed 500cc racer that Malcom Uphill had virtually written off in the Ulster Grand Prix.

Maurice Knight, who was responsible for much of the slick organisation of the Suzuki racing in the seventies, was reluctant to let me have the wrecked bike on the grounds that it would cost his company something in the region of £2,000 to have it properly repaired. I volunteered to put it back into shape, a selfish attitude, because I wanted that machine for myself.

As I loaded the bits and twisted frame into my van, Maurice called out, 'We don't want to see a huge bill when you've finished it.'

After rebuilding it to almost its original condition, I phoned Maurice to tell him the cost.

'How much is it?' he enquired rather anxiously.

'You had better wait until you see the bill,' I told him, enjoying the suspense he must have been suffering. 'It's quite substantial.'

'I knew it. I knew it would cost us a fortune,' he exclaimed.

'Well,' I said, 'it's £36 for the fibre-glass, tubing and bits and bobs. And that's the lot.'

It all went quiet at his end of the phone and I thought he was numb with disbelief. If anyone had seen the mangled wreck of a bike, they would never had thought it was possible to restore anything from it. But, to this day, Maurice has never allowed me to forget that incident.

Today's deal with Suzuki, of course, involves far more than just racing for them. Primarily, I am contracted to do Grands Prix and major international meetings at home and abroad and my aim is to win another world championship within the five years of the initial agreement with my new employers.

In December '82, when I rode into the BBC Wood Lane studios on an '82 Suzuki racer and revealed to the millions watching the Sports Personality of the Year Awards that I had switched manufacturers, the secret planning that had gone on beforehand to obtain maximum publicity proved extremely worthwhile. I had deliberately kept away from the Heron Suzuki offices in Crawley to prevent anyone learning of the new tie-up. Even my phone calls to Peter Agg and Denys Rohan were conducted in a cloak-and-dagger style that had me giving false names to the switchboard girl whom I knew from the past.

The other part of the Suzuki deal, ensuring my complete financial security virtually for life, was intended to be announced with the same explosive world-wide effect in '83. Plans were kept so quiet that my own publicity agents knew nothing until they picked up the newspapers the following day. We wanted to prevent any chance of leaks to the press which might dilute the impact.

Since the Silverstone crash, life has become increasingly good for me. While some might have doubted whether any company would maintain faith in me because of my multiple injuries, I never once contemplated difficulties over riding again provided I had good support behind me.

Now Suzuki's terms are so good I didn't even have to think about searching for a major sponsor to fund my racing team. There was no need to make any sacrifices. The team set-up was planned to be as professional as before, and without the worries of losing out at world championship rounds, we could approach each meeting in a more relaxed state of mind. In fact, as early as the winter of '82/'83 I had ordered the biggest transporter racing had ever seen: the mid-engined DAF coach, which offered increased working and living accommodation for my mechanics.

But this long-term deal with Suzuki offered the attraction of giving me other interests once I retire from bike racing. When the day to quit the sport arrives, I'll recognise it instantly. It will be when racing no longer holds any appeal for me. And it will happen probably when I'm 36.